Language Teaching:
A Scheme for Teacher Education

Editors: C N Candlin and H G Widdowson

Roles of
Teachers and Learners

Tony Wright

Oxford University Press

...iversity Press
.. Street, Oxford OX2 6DP

.xford   New York   Toronto
Delhi   Bombay   Calcutta   Madras   Karachi
Petaling Jaya   Singapore   Hong Kong   Tokyo
Nairobi   Dar es Salaam   Cape Town
Melbourne   Auckland

and associated companies in
Berlin Ibadan

OXFORD is a trade mark of Oxford University Press

ISBN 0 19 437133 6

First published 1987
Second impression 1988

© Oxford University Press 1987

Typeset in Bristol, England by Wyvern Typesetting Ltd.
Printed in Hong Kong.

For Linda, Timothy, and Elizabeth

Contents

Acknowledgements

My thanks to Chris Candlin and Henry Widdowson for their advice and support while I was working on this project. My thanks, too, to all my students who have helped me discuss many of the ideas and tasks in this book. My deepest thanks, finally, to my wife, Linda, who did some of the typing of the manuscript and helped in so many ways to ease the burden of the work.

The publishers would like to thank the following for their permission to reproduce material that falls within their copyright:

Allen and Unwin for extracts from *Towards the Creative Teaching of English* (1980) edited by L. Spaventa.

Cambridge University Press for extracts from *Functions of English* (1981) and *Ideas* (1984) by L. Jones; *Meanings Into Words* (1983) by A. Doff, C. Jones, and K. Mitchell; *Speaking Personally* (1983) by G. Porter Ladousse; *Cambridge English Course* (1985) by M. Swan and C. Walter; *The Mind's Eye* (1980) by A. Maley, A. Duff, and F. Grellet; *Grammar Games* (1984) by M. Rinvolucri; and *Keep Talking* (1984) by F. Klippel.

William Collins for an extract from *Teaching English as an International Language* (1981) by G. Abbott and J. Wingard.

The Estates Bursar, University College Oxford; Network Design, London and The London Wildlife Trust for newspaper advertisements (*The Guardian* 10.7.86, 7.7.86, and 9.7.86).

Hodder & Stoughton Educational for an extract from *Advance Your English* (1984) by R. G. Lewis.

Richard and Sally Greenhill for the photograph on page 54.

Longman Group for extracts from *Challenges* (1981) by B. Abbs, C. Candlin, C. Edelhoff, T. Moston, and M. Sexton; *Panorama* (1982) by R. Williams; *Developing Strategies* (1979) by B. Abbs and I. Freebairn; and *Kernel Lessons Intermediate* (1971) by R. O'Neill, R. Kingsbury, T. Yeadon, and R. Scott.

Macmillan, London and Basingstoke for an extract from *The Words You Need* (1981) by B. Rudzka, J. Channell, Y. Putseys, and P. Ostyn.

J. Millington-Ward for an extract from *Practice in Structure and Usage* (Longman 1972).

Thomas Nelson for an extract from *What's the Problem?* (1982) by T. Hedge and H. Dobinson.

Oxford University Press for extracts from *A Practical English Grammar Exercises 1* (1980) by A. J. Thomson and A. V. Martinet; *Fast Forward* (1986) by V. Black, M. McNorton, A. Malderez, and S. Parker; *Reading and Thinking in English: Discovering Discourse* (1979) edited by H. G. Widdowson; and *Challenge to Think* (1982) by C. Frank, M. Rinvolucri, and M. Berer.

Van Nostrand Reinhold for a figure from *Toward a Psychology of Being* (1968) by A. H. Maslow.

The author and series editors

Tony Wright is an English language teacher and teacher-trainer. He has taught English and trained teachers in West and Central Africa, the Middle East, and in Britain. At present he works for the ELT Unit at Christ Church College, Canterbury where he teaches on a variety of programmes such as general English courses, and Diploma and MA courses. His main professional interests are in the social and psychological aspects of the foreign-language classroom and in the cross-cultural implications and problems of foreign-language learning.

Christopher N. Candlin is Professor of Linguistics in the School of English and Linguistics at Macquarie University, Sydney, having previously been Professor of Applied Linguistics and Director of the Centre for Language in Social Life at the University of Lancaster. He also co-founded and directed the Institute for English Language Education at Lancaster, where he worked on issues in in-service education for teachers.

Henry Widdowson is Professor of English for Speakers of Other Languages at the University of London Institute of Education, having previously been Lecturer in Applied Linguistics at the University of Edinburgh. Before that, he worked on materials development and teacher education as a British Council English Language Officer in Sri Lanka and Bangladesh.

Through work with The British Council, The Council of Europe, and other agencies, both Editors have had extensive and varied experience of language teaching, teacher education, and curriculum development overseas, and both contribute to seminars, conferences, and professional journals.

Introduction

Roles of Teachers and Learners

The purpose of this book is to explore the ways in which role influences the teaching/learning process. Many different and complex factors influence the roles that teachers and learners adopt in the classroom. An appreciation of these factors is essential if we are to understand teaching and learning activities. Although often the social and psychological factors inherent in the roles are hidden, the process of learning a language in the classroom is underpinned by this teacher/learner relationship. It is further enriched by the part played by learning materials and the types of role implicit in the materials that are used.

We begin our investigations in the classroom and see what evidence there is of role behaviour in the extracts that follow. They are both descriptions of classroom language learning activity.

As you read them, consider the following:

> Are the activities described similar to the sorts of activity that you use in your classrooms?
> What do the teachers contribute to the activities described?
> What do the learners contribute to the activities described?
> What evidence is there that teachers and learners are working in harmony in the activities described?
> Is there any evidence of a mismatch between teacher and learner contributions to the activities?
> In what way do any of the activities differ from your own classroom?
> Would you describe either of these classrooms as 'ideal'?

Classroom 1

From the classroom across the way comes the sound of voices. The lesson has already begun. As our observers settle down, they hear the class repeating sentences in the new language in chorus, imitating the pronunciation and intonation of the teacher. They are learning the various utterances in a dialogue based on an everyday incident in the life of a student in the country where the language is spoken. Some sketches illustrating the meaning of the sentences the students are repeating have been drawn on the chalkboard. The students are not looking at these clues, but are intent on watching the lip movements and the expressions of the teacher. From time to time, however, individual students will glance at the sketches as if to reassure themselves that they really understand the meaning of what they are saying. The students' textbooks are closed.

When a pair of sentences is being repeated well in chorus, the teacher asks halves of the class to repeat this section, one in response to the other. When these smaller groups are repeating well, he asks the students to repeat the sentences by rows. Since the sentences seem now to be well memorized, the teacher calls on individuals to repeat the new sentences, sometimes in association with sentences learnt the previous day. If the individuals falter, the teacher returns to interchanges between small groups or reverts to choral repetition until the difficult part has been mastered . . .
(Rivers 1981: 4–5)

Classroom 2
The [. . .] instructor [. . .] was drilling the class in the difference between the 'present simple' and the 'present continuous'. There were twenty very thin, very eager boys aged between fourteen and twenty-two. They had been trained to compete continually against each other, so that the lesson turned into a kind of noisy greyhound race. The moment the instructor was half-way through a question, his voice was drowned by shouts of 'Teacher! Teacher! Teacher!' and I lost sight of him behind a thicket of urgently raised hands. If a student began to stumble over an answer, the others fought to grab the question for themselves, bellowing for Teacher's attention. [. . .]

The drill centred on two oilcloth pictures which had been hung on the blackboard . . .
(Raban 1979: 239)

In both of the classes described above and generally in classrooms, participants, teachers and learners alike, adopt *roles*. Through their *behaviour* in the classroom they express these roles. For example, the types of response that learners give to teachers' directions and the types of task and question that teachers pose for learners are evidence of a distinctive set of relationships. Working patterns and even seating patterns are also relevant to our understanding of these relationships.

It is unlikely that your classroom is exactly like either of those described above, but the questions you have already asked and answered are the first steps in an investigation of teacher/learner role.

The key questions to carry forward are as follows:
> What social and psychological factors contribute to the task of teaching?
> What social and psychological factors contribute to the task of learning?
> How do the two tasks interrelate socially and psychologically?

This book in common with others in the scheme consists of three sections. Section One *defines* social roles and considers factors influencing teacher and learner roles. Section Two *describes* teacher and learner roles in the classroom. In Section Three the reader can then *explore* the ideas and practices considered in the previous sections so that the extent of their relevance and feasibility can be evaluated in the actual process of teaching. The tasks which are proposed here, with their clear specification of aims and procedures and kinds of evaluation required, are designed to enable the reader to investigate teacher and learner roles in their own classrooms. *Note*: In this book, learners and teachers are referred to as 'he', 'him', etc. for stylistic convenience. These are intended as unmarked forms.

Tony Wright

Language Teaching:
A Scheme for Teacher Education

The purpose of this scheme of books is to engage language teachers in a process of continual professional development. We have designed it so as to guide teachers towards the critical appraisal of ideas and the informed application of these ideas in their own classrooms. The scheme provides the means for teachers to take the initiative themselves in pedagogic planning. The emphasis is on critical enquiry as a basis for effective action.

We believe that advances in language teaching stem from the independent efforts of teachers in their own classrooms. This independence is not brought about by imposing fixed ideas and promoting fashionable formulas. It can only occur where teachers, individually or collectively, explore principles and experiment with techniques. Our purpose is to offer guidance on how this might be achieved.

The scheme consists of three sub-series of books covering areas of enquiry and practice of immediate relevance to language teaching and learning. Sub-series 1 focuses on areas of *language knowledge*, with books linked to the conventional levels of linguistic description: pronunciation, vocabulary, grammar, and discourse. Sub-series 2 focuses on different *modes of behaviour* which realize this knowledge. It is concerned with the pedagogic skills of speaking, listening, reading, and writing. Sub-series 3 (of which this present volume forms a part) focuses on a variety of *modes of action* which are needed if this knowledge and behaviour is to be acquired in the operation of language teaching. The books in this sub-series have to do with such topics as syllabus design, the content of language courses, and aspects of methodology, and evaluation.

This sub-division of the field is not meant to suggest that different topics can be dealt with in isolation. On the contrary, the concept of a scheme implies making coherent links between all these different areas of enquiry and activity. We wish to emphasize how their integration formalizes the complex factors present in any teaching process. Each book, then, highlights a particular topic, but also deals contingently with other issues, themselves treated as focal in other books in the series. Clearly, an enquiry into a mode of behaviour like speaking, for example, must also refer to aspects of language knowledge which it realizes. It must also connect to modes of action which can be directed at developing this behaviour in learners. As elements of the whole scheme, therefore, books cross-refer both within and across the different sub-series.

This principle of cross-reference which links the elements of the scheme is also applied to the internal design of the different inter-related books within it. Thus, each book contains three sections, which, by a combination of text and task, engage the reader in a principled enquiry into ideas and practices. The first section of each book makes explicit those theoretical ideas which bear on the topic in question. It provides a conceptual framework for those sections which follow. Here the text has a mainly *explanatory* function, and the tasks serve to clarify and consolidate the points raised. The second section shifts the focus of attention to how the ideas from Section One relate to activities in the classroom. Here the text is concerned with *demonstration*, and the tasks are designed to get readers to evaluate suggestions for teaching in reference both to the ideas from Section One and also to their own teaching experience. In the third section this experience is projected into future work. Here the set of tasks, modelled on those in Section Two, are designed to be carried out by the reader as a combination of teaching techniques and action research in the actual classroom. It is this section that renews the reader's contact with reality: the ideas expounded in Section One and linked to pedagogic practice in Section Two are now to be systematically *tested out* in the process of classroom teaching.

If language teaching is to be a genuinely professional enterprise, it requires continual experimentation and evaluation on the part of practitioners whereby in seeking to be more effective in their pedagogy they provide at the same time — and as a corollary — for their own continuing education. It is our aim in this scheme to promote this dual purpose.

Christopher N. Candlin
Henry Widdowson

Teaching and learning as social activities

1 What is a role?

The *Concise Oxford Dictionary* (1982) defines 'role' as:

> actor's part; one's function, what person or thing is appointed or expected to do.

In our daily lives, we fulfil roles that have features of all these defining characteristics. We are, in a multitude of ways, actors of *social roles*.

We have roles in society – we play parts in society. These differ: some roles are hard to avoid (e.g. father); some roles may be thrust upon us by circumstances (e.g. school pupil); on the other hand, we choose for ourselves many of the roles we fulfil (e.g. teacher).

Whatever the case, once we are placed or place ourselves in a role, others will expect certain types of behaviour of us.

Actors and social actors

Although we 'play parts' in society, the parts differ from an actor's roles in several ways as well as being similar in others. For instance, once an actor is cast in a certain role, he cannot change it. The role is restricted to the range of behaviour and the place in the drama that the writer has chosen for that role. Thus an actor plays 'hero' or 'villain' within the framework already laid down by the writer. Despite this restriction, theatrical roles are open to interpretation in much the same way as we are able to interpret our social roles.

However, our 'life roles' are more flexible and fluid. In a drama, the same lines will always be spoken; in life, we rarely if ever play out our roles in precisely the same way on every occasion. Circumstances change. None the less, we can discern patterns of behaviour in social roles.

1.1 Defining social roles

If we pick up a newspaper and read, at random, reports on various events, we commonly find people identified by both their name *and* occupation. In the extracts below, the occupational 'roles' are in bold.

> Dr Prem Misra, **Consultant Psychiatrist** at Duke Street Hospital in Glasgow, revealed that he has treated four teenage boys after they became computer addicts . . .

and

> *The Daily Mirror* will resume production tonight after Mr Robert

Maxwell, **publisher** of Mirror Group Newspapers, struck a settlement with the National Graphical Association print union.

When a person's name is very well-known, only the 'role' is mentioned. For example:

The Prime Minister has decided not to bring Mr Cecil Parkinson back into her government . . .
(*The Guardian* 2.9.85)

Superficially, occupations seem to define social roles and, in most societies, the chief defining characteristic of a role is the occupational aspect. However, there are other features which define roles. In order to discuss these, let us take an example – an airline pilot.

Doing

Picture the uniformed pilot sitting at the controls of his aircraft. In this position, he operates the controls, reads the instruments and performs various manoeuvres such as taking off and landing, climbing, cruising, and turning. The pilot flies the aircraft.

Talking

He is not alone though. In the cockpit he talks to the co-pilot, navigator, and engineer about various technical aspects of flying the plane. He also communicates with ground stations in order to give details of the flight and to ask for information and assistance, among other things. Flying a plane also involves talking to people; although the pilot makes decisions, he relies on others to help him reach these decisions, simply because he is unable to be in possession of all the information he needs at any one time.

More than one role

The pilot does not only fly the plane; he is also captain. He is at the head of a chain of command which is responsible for the smooth operation of the aircraft's functions as restaurant, cinema, and dormitory – the aircraft, too, has many roles. As captain, he is ultimately responsible for the safety of the passengers. The two roles overlap here – the plane has to be flown safely and the pilot has to react to unforeseen emergencies such as mechanical failure or bad weather conditions. The captain has to react to emergencies – in the extreme, a hijacking – which may endanger the passengers. Both roles involve human contact, but of differing types.

Expectations

In order to test out some of your ideas about an airline pilot's roles, now imagine you are a passenger on a plane. It so happens that the pilot is a young man in his twenties, with uncombed hair, dirty clothes, and wearing sandals. When he comes out of the cockpit during the flight, an unlit handrolled cigarette hangs from his mouth and he has a can of beer in his hand. He proceeds to make passes at all the young women on the flight, including the stewardesses. He then returns to the cockpit and, over the intercom, denounces the political rulers of his country and the management of the company which employs him.

Would you panic? Would you be outraged? Would you lose confidence in the pilot's ability to fly the plane smoothly? Would your *expectations* of the pilot be disappointed? It is likely that they would.

In short, *there is more to a role than just doing a job*! Furthermore, the role in question is governed both by our expectations and the *actual behaviour* of the pilot. The two are very closely related. The fact that our pilot has certain social habits and political views *should* be irrelevant to his function as a pilot. But we probably expect him to be politically neutral on duty, to wear the standard uniform and behave in a 'professional' manner towards the passengers and crew. Any behaviour that is not detached, impersonal and cool might prevent him from flying the plane safely. We expect a pilot to be a pilot.

▶ ## TASK 1

We have seen the sort of behaviour that a pilot might indulge in which is contrary to our expectations. Can you now draw up a scenario in which a teacher is behaving contrary to expectations? By doing so, you will clarify your own expectations of a teacher's 'in-role' behaviour.

When you have done this, do the same for the learner.

Remember to think of the 'work' teachers and learners traditionally have to do and how they communicate.

We have identified the main role-defining characteristics of an airline pilot. You have, by constructing the 'anti-teacher' and 'anti-learner', done the same for teacher and learner. The main characteristics of a social role are:

1 The *work done* and *job-related* activities.
2 The *relationships* and *communications* they have with others. These help to define the role more clearly.
3 *Beliefs* and *attitudes*.

You may also consider that the *use of a uniform, sex, age,* and any *special abilities* further define the role. These do not necessarily affect behaviour, however.

▶ ## TASK 2

Now examine the list of occupations and social positions below. For each one, note down your expectations as to their role behaviour according to the characteristics of role discussed.

father	grandparent	librarian	mechanic
mother	judge	teacher	civil servant
uncle	bus driver	priest	journalist
son	accountant	doctor	
daughter	salesman	detective	

In defining each role, which do you think is the most important defining characteristic? (work, personal relationships, uniform, etc.)

Divide the list into two groups: those roles which are primarily defined by the work done and those which are mainly defined by the importance of the quality of the interpersonal relationships.

What do you think are the critical differences between the family roles (father, etc.) and the others?

Which roles do you think are closest to the role of teacher and which closest to the role of learner? What reasons can you give for your choice?

Behind our expectations of role behaviour there lies a set of attitudes and beliefs about the roles in question. When an individual acts out of role as in the case of the airline pilot or the teacher and learner you constructed in Task 1, they are not matching with our expectations. Our beliefs and attitudes also contribute to our expectations of what is *normal* behaviour. We can say that the roles *interlock* when both sets of expectations mirror each other.

How far do you think that your cultural beliefs have influenced your work in Task 2?

How much do you think your cultural beliefs affect your expectations of role behaviour?

1.2 Role sets and role networks

When individuals are acting 'in role' they communicate with each other in specific ways. In many organizations, the channels of communication are standardized and even ritualized in order to avoid out-of-role behaviour. For example, the pilot's functional channels of communication, to do with flying the aircraft, are clear and unambiguous: all messages must be understood. In this way the aircraft and its occupants are safeguarded.

There is also an organizational *network* among the crew. Communication patterns conform to this network for the purposes of flying the plane. The aircraft performs its many functions properly because of the collective acceptance of the chain of command. The network looks something like this:

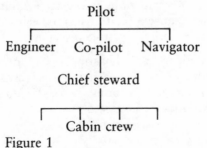

Figure 1

The network only shows us the relationships between the personnel in respect of the jobs they do. How the crew relate to each other as people, whether they like or dislike each other for instance, is another matter. The permutations of possible relationships between the members of an aircraft crew are endless. These relationships are at a personal rather than an institutional level and give us an impression of whether the organization is 'happy' or not. The pilot is also a member of a wider social grouping known as a *role set*. To a large extent, the pilot's role is defined by his membership of this role set. It looks like this:

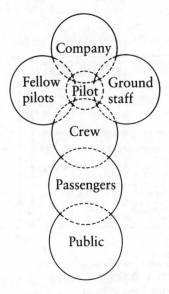

Figure 2

Role can, therefore, be defined from several different standpoints. We are interested in the job or *task-related* aspects of role and the *interpersonal* aspects of role, too. We are also interested in how these relate to each other.

Role is a complex grouping of factors which combine to produce certain types of social behaviour.

▶ **TASK 3**

We have looked at the role network and the role set of the airline pilot. Both, as we noted, contribute to the role behaviour of the individual.

1 Map out the role set and the role network of a teacher and a learner.
- Make a list of all the people with whom a teacher and a learner may have contact in the establishment where you work.
- Make a second list of the people outside the school itself who influence the behaviour of teachers and learners.

2 Now draw diagrams of the same type as those for the airline pilot:
- for the organization of the school – the teacher's and learner's role network
- for the wider community – the teacher's and learner's role set.

3 Are the relationships hierarchical?

4 Who most directly influences the behaviour of teacher and learner?

▶ TASK 4

Study these job advertisements and then do the following task:

RECRUITMENT CONSULTANT

(Graphic Design)   Salary to £15K

Network Design is one of London's leading established specialists in the recruitment of talented creative individuals with the Graphic and Interior Design market.

Due to our successful expansion in this area, we are looking for another lively Consultant with ideally a Sales or Design background, and who is likely to be aged in his/her early 20s to join us.

All applicants will be treated in the strictest confidence and full cv should be sent to:

Stuart Newman
NETWORK DESIGN (Rec Cons)
Grosvenor Gardens House
35/37 Grosvenor Gardens
London SW1W 0BS

7/7/86

The London Wildlife Trust
requires

CONTRACT SURVEY ORGANISER

LWT attracts an increasing number of area and site surveys for local authorities and other bodies. We need an enthusiastic person with botanical survey experience to: oversee and implement, undertake and sub-contract work.

We are looking for an ability to cost & negotiate for contracts, administer substantial budgets, and to expand the Trust's contract.

Salary: initially £8,500. Apply with C.V. to LWT (CSO), 80 York Way, London N1 9AG.

LWT is an equal opportunity employer. Non-smoking office.

9/7/86

UNIVERSITY COLLEGE, OXFORD

DOMESTIC BURSARSHIP

The college proposes to appoint a Domestic Bursar, with general responsibility for the domestic administration of the college, to take up the position in October, 1986, or as soon as possible thereafter. The post carries with it eligibility for an Official Fellowship.

Applications should be addressed to: The Estates Bursar (from whom further particulars may be obtained), before August 1, 1986.

10/7/86

All advertisements from
The Guardian (dates of publication included)

1 identify and note the various characteristics of each job;

2 decide how the jobs differ in terms of expected role behaviour – is the job task- or interpersonally-oriented?

3 predict the likely nature of the interpersonal relationships within each. Would the organization be hierarchical, for example? Would the relationships with work fellows be formal or informal?

4 predict 'hidden' roles within each job;

5 decide on a ranking for the jobs from most to least task-oriented.

1.3 Some problems associated with role

Imagine someone taking a new job. In the early stages of coming to terms with the new roles that the job entails, there are likely to be problems if the individual is not fully prepared for the job or is not certain how to behave. The occurrence of these problems further defines the role in question, enabling us to pin down more closely our expectations of the normal behaviour associated with the role.

Sometimes an individual may find it extremely difficult to define or 'understand' his role. The result will be behaviour that is contrary to people's expectations – it is somehow inconsistent. For example, when starting a new job or changing a family role, an individual is likely to be disoriented or uncertain of how to behave. This can lead to poor relations with others, ineffectiveness in the task-oriented aspects of the role, or just plain unhappiness on the part of the individual. On a more positive note, recognition of the problem often leads to behaviour which attempts to resolve it.

As we saw, there are two major aspects of an airline pilot's role – the task-oriented and the interpersonal. If these two aspects cannot be kept separate, *conflict* is likely to arise. Thus it would be unusual if the captain addressed the chief cabin steward about catering arrangements in the sort of language normally used when communicating with group control. Further conflict may be caused by *overlapping* roles. How 'professional', for instance, would the relationship between pilot and navigator be if they were brothers?

Major conflict can also occur when the personality of the individual is at odds with the role. For example, a taciturn, suspicious individual is unlikely to be a good salesman, and gregarious people are unlikely to be happy in jobs which entail working alone.

Within the role itself there may be conflicting *pressures*. An instance of this may be where the airline pilot is responsible for enforcing a company labour relations policy that neither the crew nor he likes. But because of his role, he has to enforce the policy.

Think about these problems from the teacher's and learner's points of view.
    Can you think of instances of overlapping roles for either teacher or learner?
    Can you think of instances when the personality of either teacher or learner is at odds with the role?
    Can you note any pressures or conflicts inherent in either teacher or learner role?

Keep your notes for reference later in Sections One, Two, and Three.

1.4 Teachers and learners

What do we know about teacher and learner roles?

Doing: There are many different aspects of teaching and learning which are task-related. We shall examine them in detail in Section Two.

Talking: Teaching and learning are essentially social activities, implying role relationships between teacher and learner, learner and learner. These relationships are established, maintained, and evaluated through communication.

More than one role: A teacher has many roles. A teacher can be father, mother, judge, salesman, technician, librarian, and more within the role.

Beliefs: The whole educational process is deeply influenced by beliefs and attitudes. All those members of the teacher's and learner's role sets have beliefs and attitudes which influence the teaching/learning process.

Special abilities: Society may hold the view that special abilities and aptitudes are essential for the successful fulfilment of teacher and learner roles. Furthermore, age and sex may also be regarded as role-defining characteristics. For example, in your society, is the teacher referred to as 'he' or 'she'?

Uniform: In many educational systems roles are clearly marked by uniforms or standardized dress codes. These often complement codes of behaviour laid down for the teacher and learner roles.

Think about the following questions.
> What do you think your learners expect of you as a teacher?
> What do you think 'good education' consists of? Do you think your learners share your view?
> Do the age and sex of a teacher play a part in influencing learners' expectations of their behaviour?
> What do you think the ideal relationship between teachers and learners should be like?
> Are uniform or behaviour codes important for teachers and learners in your country?

Does any of what you have noted above match with the notes you made on the problems associated with role?

2 Factors influencing teacher and learner roles

Classroom language learning is a group activity. The nature of the activity will vary according to several factors. These influence the roles individuals adopt (or are given) in the classroom language learning process and how they interpret their roles.

In order to find out what these factors are, we need to know answers to the following:

> What do individuals contribute to a learning group?
> What do individuals do in a learning group?
> What are the effects of the group process on both individuals and groups?

These three questions are related. What individuals contribute to the group amounts to a set of expectations about how others will act and what roles they will adopt. These expectations will initially influence what actually happens in the group. Initial expectations and behaviour will be modified according to the duration and quality of the group's activities.

The social and psychological 'baggage' that participants bring with them naturally influences the actions of the group – roles are adopted and distributed on the basis of these factors. During the group's activity, people may modify their behaviour and change their roles in the light of the contributions of others. This in itself will create new conditions, and modify expectations. Knowledge will be gained or modified as time progresses and the activity unfolds. Quite simply, group activity is dynamic.

Conditions within the group are constantly changing. The effects of these changes are cumulative. At the end of a group activity such as a lesson, we might be in a position to say, 'Well – this has changed, that has not changed.' However, we must always bear in mind that teaching/learning activity is a long-term process, and the changes in participants' behaviour and knowledge are usually difficult to evaluate and measure.

We are concerned with how initial expectations about roles contribute to the group process and also how teachers' and learners' behaviour contributes to the classroom language learning process. We also need to know how the group process might bring about changes in behaviour over the long term. We must also bear in mind that roles are likely to change because group activity is dynamic. We have to conceive of roles as flexible and dynamic too.

Initial contributions to group activity

We shall divide the factors into two broad groups.

1 Social and psychological factors. These include views about status and position, attitudes and values held by individuals and groups and individuals' personalities. (Interpersonal aspects of role.)

2 Teachers' and learners' expectations about the nature of learning tasks and the way in which individuals and groups deal with learning tasks. (Task-related aspects of role.)

The two sets of factors relate closely to the interpersonal and task-related aspects of role we have already identified.

2.1 Interpersonal factors

Social role and status

In most societies, the social roles of teacher and learner are accorded high and low status respectively. This differential relationship has many implications for what can happen in the classroom.

Role and status imply a set of power relationships.

Role and status also confer on their holders a set of rights, duties, and obligations.

Social distance results from differing status and position.

Status and position have a great influence on the sorts of role a teacher or learner may fulfil. They underpin all role behaviour.

Status depends on the amount of esteem, admiration, and approval we get from our immediate social group, as well as society in general. The fact that one becomes a parent is enough to convey status in many societies, for example. Detailed studies of the phenomenon of status indicate that the amount of esteem, admiration, and approval we receive depends on such criteria as wealth (hence, *status symbols* which cost a great deal) and intelligence (it seems to be acknowledged that certain occupations can only be performed by 'intelligent' people). There is thus a relationship between the markers of status and the rewards associated with status, and its achievement. Status, it seems, has to be 'won' unless one is fortunate enough to be born into a family already holding high status.

There is a subtle difference between status and *position* that we must also note. The position of 'Head of Languages' or similar in a large school may be enough in itself to confer on the holder of the post a certain amount of status – he is 'in charge' of the language programmes at the school. But while the position itself does not change, status can vary. Unless the organization of the school is changed, there will always be a Head of Languages. But an unsuccessful Head of Languages will not be accorded the same high status as a popular or highly successful holder of the position, either from society at large or his or her colleagues in the teaching profession. Status depends on what people think and feel about an individual's performance of a role. In some cases, for example, society has deemed that exam results are the criterion for success and therefore high status. Status thus depends on a social group's *norms* and *values*.

In other words, status depends on what a social group regard as normal behaviour and what they regard as having positive worth. Position, on the other hand, is almost the equivalent of the title of the job. Thus, 'teacher' is a position with a certain amount of status. In broad terms, it is the equivalent of the term 'role' as we have used it so far. As we have seen, however, role is usually many-faceted and most positions imply more than one role.

▶ TASK 5

1 We considered criteria such as wealth and intelligence in our discussion of status. What are the criteria for status *in your society*? What are the markers of status in your society? i.e. status symbols, salary, etc.

2 What do the public value in a teacher in your society? Examine the list of factors below and tick them if they apply to your society. Add any other factors to the list if you wish to.

> Excellent exam results from learners
> Many qualifications
> Good disciplinarian
> Caring, gentle attitude towards pupils
> Gets on well with colleagues
> Always willing to take on extra work
> Exemplary private life
> Accepts authority
> Writes textbooks for local use
> Others (specify)

Now put these in rank order, the most important factor first.

3 What do the public value in a learner in your society? Examine the list of factors below and tick them if they apply to your society. Add any other factors to the list if you wish to.

> Good at all subjects
> Well-behaved
> Accepts authority

> Good at sports and games
> Has a large number of hobbies
> Has a good exam record
> Respects his/her colleagues
> Others (specify)
> Now put them in rank order, the most important factor first.
>
> 4 Do you think that your students would rank the factors in 1, 2, and 3 in the same way as you have done?
>
> What differences do you perceive between your own and society's views, and between your own and your learners' views?
>
> What do you think is the significance for teachers' status of the views of the public where you work?
>
> Do you think that the ability to speak a foreign language confers high status on an individual in your society? What are the implications of this for your own status as a language teacher?

Status and position are vital influences on social role because our knowledge and perceptions of status and position contribute to our expectations of people's behaviour and influence our own behaviour when we encounter these people. It is doubtful whether learners, teachers, and the general public have similar perceptions of each other's worth and the types of performance that are valued. This complicates the role relationship between the teachers and learners and at the same time gives it some of its distinctive character.

As well as being acknowledged and rewarded with status markers as we have noted, status is also acknowledged in other ways, both verbal and non-verbal.

In many societies, status is marked by particular types of non-verbal behaviour. We may, for instance, prostrate ourselves at the feet of a superior or avert our eyes from his. Even the distance we may keep from one of high status may be governed by rules of behaviour. Position, too, is acknowledged in the same sorts of way, for instance in the armed forces when those of an inferior rank must come to attention and salute a superior. In this case, the superior rank is accorded status.

In our speech, too, we acknowledge status and position. Consider the utterance of 'Sir' or the use of expressions such as 'Your Excellency'. And in Britain, it is unusual to call one's natural father or mother by their first names, for example. On the other hand, we do not address our intimates in a formal way unless we wish to convey irony or sarcasm.

Consider, too, a typical statement by a leading public figure: 'We shall go forward together.' Why not say 'You and I' instead of 'We'? 'We' conveys an element of solidarity and collective effort. Studies of the use of pronouns in English also indicate that we can convey equality or mark higher status and position through their use.

Teachers, too, vary their ways of addressing the members of their learning group. Sometimes, first names may be used. At others, family names may be used. The interchange between the two address forms can be used to mark position and status. *In short, perceptions of status and position consistently influence how an individual behaves, both verbally and non-verbally.*

We communicate a great deal of social information about ourselves and the way we perceive others by the way we acknowledge their status and position.

▶ **TASK 6**

   1 List the ways – both verbal and non-verbal – in which status and position are acknowledged in your culture.

   2 List the ways in which teachers and learners mark their respective status and positions in your society, both verbally and non-verbally.

   What are the implications for behaviour in the classroom of the ways in which teachers and learners acknowledge each other's status in your society? Are they likely to enhance or limit the teacher/learner relationship?

Rights, duties and obligations

There are other aspects of a position which contribute to the role-behaviour of an individual. A certain position entails certain *rights, duties, and obligations*. All social positions may be seen as having certain rights, duties, and obligations attaching to them.

One's duties are closely related to the task-oriented aspect of a role. As part of the expectations linked to the role, the duties carry a certain amount of moral weight. We must be seen to have done our duty. Failure to carry out our duties usually results in the imposition of some sort of sanction.

One's rights are defined by a complex of social conventions. It is as if we have been given by society the authority or permission to do something. We are given justification for certain courses of action. Rights are usually defined relative to the rights of others in the society. What we can do by right depends on what society believes. Society may, for instance, give the teacher the right to punish a child for misbehaving.

Obligations differ subtly from both rights and duties in that obligations are usually the result of social relationships. Teachers may *feel* they have obligations towards their students but the obligations are not subject to sanctions. They rely on mutual trust and respect for their interpretation.

Another important point to note is that rights, duties, and obligations are subject to change and reinterpretation over time. This is particularly important with regard to our understanding of group activity. As groups evolve, rights, duties, and obligations may be redistributed. This is particularly true of groups of young learners growing up with their rights, duties, and obligations evolving, at the same time.

▶ ## TASK 7

Draw up lists of what you regard as your rights, duties, and obligations to your learners. You can use the list below to assist you if you wish.

> Choosing learning material
> Punishing learners' misbehaviour
> Being respected by learners
> Imposing discipline on learners
> Deciding seating arrangements in the classroom
> Setting work for learners
> Marking work done by learners
> Making rules of behaviour in class
> Deciding on the procedure for learning
> Providing knowledge for learners

Do you think any of the rights, duties, and obligations that you have noted can change as circumstances change in the learning group?

Are there some rights, duties, and obligations which would never change, regardless of circumstances?

Are there any rights, duties, and obligations that you think are inseparable from the role of the teacher? How much do you think these contribute to the expectations we have of the teacher role?

What rights, duties, and obligations to their teachers do you think learners have?

Power

Whichever way we look at the teacher/learner relationship, we have to admit that, because of the relative positions and statuses, *power* plays a large part in the relationship. Indeed, some would go so far as to say that it is the most important factor. Power, or the lack of it, is implicit in any social role. If we think of power in the sense of directing or influencing the behaviour of others, certain social roles and certain high status individuals or groups are likely to have power. Whether they choose to impose it is another matter.

The rights, duties, and obligations of teachers and learners are related to power. For example, many teachers might claim to have the right to punish learners who misbehave. A teacher's duty to provide the learners under his direction with knowledge must be balanced against this power. Many teachers believe that learners are obliged to respect them, simply because teachers hold a certain social role. All these and other factors have to be balanced if we are to see the nature of the power relationship between teachers and learners.

In any social encounter involving two or more people, there are power relationships. It is very rare, however, for power to be equally shared — *power relationships are almost always asymmetrical.* One individual is likely, for one reason or another, to have more power than another. This may be because of the relative status of the individuals or because of the way in which rights, duties, and obligations are shared among the participants.

Social psychologists distinguish between three different types of power — *coercive, reward-based,* and *referent.* What sort of power relationships between individuals are implied by these types of power?

Coercive: The basis of this sort of power is *punishment.* Some individuals and institutions have the right and thus the authority to punish others. Institutions and relationships based on this type of power are likely to be very one-sided and full of potential for confrontation. Who *wants* to go to prison, for example?

Reward-based: The basis of this type of power is *reward.* Some individuals or organizations have power to reward what they view as appropriate behaviour. Business organizations reward employees with a salary and perhaps other perks of the job, for example. Some psychologists reckon that in some families love is used as 'reward currency' in power struggles between the family members.

Referent: The basis of this type of power is *motivation.* Individuals or organizations exercising referent power are appealing to the commitment and interest of the other members. Tasks are seen as collective endeavours and thus power is used as a means of enforcing group effort.

Very few social encounters will exhibit the characteristics of only one type of power relationship. In a prison, for example, reward-based power is exercised in the form of paroles and reductions of sentence for good behaviour. Referent power is exercised through education and rehabilitation programmes.

Now let us think about the power relationships in a classroom. Study the descriptions of classroom life that follow:

A . . . It was the agonizing era of long division, of fractions, of decimals, of
simple and compound interest; of dictation, spelling, 'comprehension'
and what was eccentrically referred to as 'general knowledge'.
  – What island is known as Little England?
  'Barbados.'

— The Isle of Spices?
'Grenada.'
— A stitch in time saves what?
'Nine.'
— What do too many cooks spoil?
'The broth.'
— Spell Czechoslovakia . . .

One's knuckles would be rapped with the edge of a ruler until they were bruised and swollen, angry fists would pound the back of one's head. I recall a memorable beating in front of a blackboard chalked up with rows of fractions upon which I gazed blankly, petrified into idiocy by a leather strap . . .
(Naipaul 1984: 11–12)

B I invited six people to sit around a table, in view of the rest of the audience. When they were settled, I opened my bag of rods and dumped them onto the centre of the table. Then I picked up rods of various colours, one by one, and looked at them. Finally, I picked up one of the longer rods, motioned for everyone to listen and remain silent, and pronounced the word *cubuk* ('Rod').

After this dramatic event, I held the learners silent for a few seconds, and then motioned them to say the word in unison. When they had spoken the word chorally a few times, I picked up the same rod time after time, and had individuals pronounce the word. If one learner's pronunciation was very far different from what native speakers would have understood, I had him try it again . . .
(Stevick 1980: 53)

▶ **TASK 8**

1 What types of power does the teacher exercise in each of the extracts above?

2 Compare these extracts with those in the Introduction to Section One. Which ones seem to be relying on the imposition of coercive power? Which ones rely on reward-based power and which on referent power? What sort of rewards seem to be offered? What sort of referent power is used — reference to a group or a co-operative task?

As well as being implicit in certain social roles, power also derives from status. High status individuals whose status depends on high esteem have a better chance of successfully employing power than lower status individuals. Power is more likely to be of the referent type in these cases – hence the power of a performer over his or her audience. A person with knowledge is in a similar position, especially if the knowledge is a desirable commodity. An exercise of power might be seen in the withholding of that knowledge or the imposition of conditions on its being given.

▶ TASK 9

Can you think of any occasions when a teacher might use the threat of withdrawal of knowledge as a means of coercing his pupils to work harder? What sort of relationship do you think might exist between the teacher and his class in this case?

The type of social grouping – whether *formal* or *informal* – will also influence the way in which power can be used. Research with social groups under experimental conditions highlights the difference between those groups whose leader was appointed and those groups which established their own leadership. In the formal groups with an appointed leader, the use of rewards and punishments was most noticeable whereas, in informal groups, referent power was more freely employed. In these cases, the leaders emerged through their skills of handling others' demands and the ability to compromise. Further, these leaders were able to motivate the groups more effectively in the completion of tasks.

Think about this:

Do you think your learning group is a formal or an informal group in terms of how leadership is decided?

Keep your notes for reference in Sections Two and Three.

Social distance

We must all, at one time or another, have felt inferior or superior, or close to or distant from others in social encounters. We were probably keenly aware of the social distance that results from differing relative statuses and positions in organizations. For example, we probably feel socially distant from royalty or political leaders or even the 'boss'.

This feeling of social distance is modified by the degree of formality or informality under which the social encounter takes place. The more informal and relaxed the situation is, the greater the likelihood of a lowering of social distance. On the other hand, we may wish for a more formal situation, so that we are not forced into lowering social distance. If social distance is lowered, we become more intimate and are more likely to reveal things about ourselves.

In groups of people, social distance is less when there are common interests which are shared. A final example is of the foreigner visiting a country for the first time. He may feel 'distant' from those he meets and suffer from what is called 'culture shock' or alienation.

Teachers and learners are also subject to social distance. The reasons for this are as follows:

> differing ages
> differing interests
> different levels of knowledge about the subject being learnt
> unequal status
> unequal distribution of power
> in some cases, different cultures.

Would you add any that are specific to your own culture?

Now think about your own teaching situation.

> Do you think that there is a high or low level of social distance between you and your learners?
> What evidence would you use to support your answer?
> Do you think that the level of social distance varies according to different teaching/learning activities or do you think it stays more or less the same whatever the activity?

All our social behaviour exhibits evidence of a knowledge of social distance. For example, we are polite to perceived superiors. We also defer to social superiors and let them 'have their way'; a challenge to the superior individual's status would be regarded as impolite. Think about the following question:

> How are learners in your teaching situation required to acknowledge the social distance between them and their teachers? Is it done verbally or non-verbally, or both? Give examples.

Power and social distance usually combine in social encounters to produce certain sorts of behaviour. Power is measured as $+P$ or $-P$, depending on whether it is imposed or not; that choice remains with the powerful individual. Distance is measured as $+D$ or $-D$ to show whether it is high or low.

Let us look at an example to see how this might work.
Situation: two total strangers from different countries meet in a hotel at which they are guests.

$$-P +D$$

There is no power relationship between them on first meeting: they are equals. However, there is considerable social distance.

▶ TASK 10

> Examine the classroom situations which follow and decide on the power and distance relations between teachers and learners.

Say whether they are +**P** or −**P**, depending on whether or not the power is actually imposed by the powerful participant, and +**D** or −**D**, according to whether or not you think there is likely to be high or low social distance between the teachers and learners.

1 The teacher is advising a learner on the choice of extra reading material. The learner is considerably younger than the teacher.
2 A new teacher enters the class for the first time and tells the learners to get their textbooks out and sit in their places.
3 The teacher relates a personal anecdote to illustrate a vocabulary point.
4 The teacher corrects a learner's faulty pronunciation.
5 The teacher invites an evaluation of a new piece of teaching material from the learners.
6 The teacher asks the learners to form small groups for an activity.
7 The teacher admits making a mistake to the class.
8 A learner asks the teacher for clarification of a grammar point after the teacher has explained it.
9 The learners spontaneously start discussing a point raised by the teacher. The teacher joins in the discussion.

On the basis of your decisions about **P** and **D** in the scenarios above, divide them into two groups. The first set should be those with a low distance factor and the second with a high power factor.

Can you make any general statements about the sort of atmosphere that each tendency towards **P** or **D** might create and what sorts of teacher/learner relationship would arise?

The nature of the role relationship between teacher and learner is not static, either. Just as status can be won through achievement, so power and distance can vary in the course of a single lesson. Different teaching strategies and different learning activities lead to modifications of the initial power/distance equation. For example, scenarios 3, 4, and 8 could all occur in one single lesson. Look back at the way you have computed **P** and **D** in those scenarios and see if you agree with the idea that power and distance vary.

Attitudes and beliefs

Our attitudes towards other individuals and the social groups they represent are a very important aspect of the psychological 'baggage' we bring with us to social encounters such as the classroom. Our attitudes may influence how much social distance we feel or choose to keep and whether or not we choose to impose power on others. They contribute greatly to our expectations of others' behaviour in certain role relationships.

The way in which we interpret our role and the role of another individual depends on our attitudes and beliefs about the roles themselves and the individuals who occupy them.

Think about these questions:

How do we form attitudes and beliefs?
How do we make our attitudes and beliefs known?
What is the relevance of this area for teachers?
Why is it necessary to consider these points?

Values
Our social group or peer group may value trust more highly than intelligence. As an individual you may value sympathy more highly than the ability to make money. Such values are formed by a complex process of interaction with our social environment, particularly during childhood and adolescence.

Values take a long time to form. They also take a long time to change once they are established. *Our values are the basis for our attitudes.* We value things and people positively or negatively; we have positive, negative or neutral attitudes towards these people and things. Our attitudes affect our behaviour.

In social life, we are constantly expressing positive and negative attitudes. We need to know how we do this and which aspects of our behaviour clearly express attitudes.

Attitudes can be expressed both verbally and non-verbally. On a simple level if we say that some event 'is a good thing' we are expressing a positive attitude towards it. If we do not show a willingness to do something we have been asked to, we may be said to show a negative attitude.

Beliefs differ from attitudes. A belief can be verbalized, whereas an attitude is 'hidden' and also much more complex. An attitude can be expressed by a range of behaviour; a belief can only be expressed verbally. Both our attitudes and beliefs are influenced by our values.

The next three tasks are designed to assist you in exploring your own attitudes and values.

▶ **TASK 11**

Examine the statements which follow. They express beliefs about social behaviour in educational settings.

We should address each other by first names.
We should not show anger in front of another person.
People are basically well intentioned.
People must not criticize each other in public.

We should respect another's privacy.
We should all develop as human beings.
We should always attempt to do our best.
We should respect our superiors.
All people have roughly the same level of intelligence.
We should respect another person's opinion on an issue.
The teacher's job is to give knowledge.
The learner's job is to absorb the knowledge teachers give them.

Now consider the following questions:

1 Which of these beliefs do you subscribe to?
2 What sort of values do you think inform such beliefs?
3 How much do you think your perception of status influences your
   beliefs?
4 Do you think that you hold professional attitudes and beliefs in
   common with your fellow teachers?

▶ TASK 12

1 Look at the list of non-verbal elements of social interaction
   below. For each one, decide how you could express a positive or
   negative attitude towards another person.

      bodily contact
      closeness (proximity)
      posture (how we stand or sit)
      facial expression
      gesture
      direction of gaze
      tone of voice

2 How far do you think your answers to this task are a reflection of
   your own sociocultural background?

Attitudes in common
One feature of social groups is that they hold beliefs and attitudes in
common. They all tend to believe in roughly the same things and to value
the same things positively or negatively.

All people have strong desires to belong to a group. They need to *identify*
themselves with others, to feel the same way about things as they do.

Social psychologists have devoted a great deal of time to research on
commonly-held beliefs and attitudes because they perceive their powerful
influence on role behaviour and our expectations regarding the behaviour
of others.

▶ **TASK 13**

In order to help you clarify your values and to think about your attitudes towards other people, teaching, and your learners, respond to the statements below.
Be as honest as you can!

If you are working with a colleague or group, you may like to share your feelings. The discussion could be very valuable.

We should not disclose personal information and feelings to a close friend.
We should never visit another person socially unannounced.
We should not swear in the company of others.
We should not talk to a close friend about religion or politics.
We should inform our intimates about our schedules.
We should not tease another person.
We should respect an intimate friend regardless of their faults.
We should criticize the learners' work constructively.
We should discipline learners when necessary.
We should always take our learners' work seriously.
We should admit we are wrong when we have to.
We should not supervise learners' work too closely.
We should pay attention to learners' personal problems.

Learners should hand in their work on time.
Learners should always acknowledge the teacher's authority.
Learners must always be polite to teachers.
(Based on Henderson and Argyle 1984)

Teachers and learners
Teachers and learners have beliefs and attitudes about each other when cast in these roles. These beliefs and attitudes directly and indirectly affect their expectations about classroom behaviour.

We can see how beliefs can affect behaviour by looking at the different stages of personal and cognitive development that a learner might go through and how these stages might reflect beliefs. (See Perry 1968.)

1 'Black and white': at this stage of development, the learner sees the world in terms of good and bad, black and white. Authority rests with the teacher who is assumed to 'know the answers'.

2 'Everything is relative': the learner now accepts the potential diversity of belief and concept, and can perceive that everything is relative – at this stage, it is easier for the learner to see another person's point of view.

3 'Commitment': the learner can now commit himself to an idea or concept. Thus, learning a foreign language could be seen as a means of realizing one's true identity or worth.

Learners at different stages are likely to prefer different ways of learning. At stage 1 learners may only be confident enough in their ability to memorize facts about language which could be judged right or wrong. At stages 2 and 3 they are more likely to think independently and to prefer problem-solving as a means of learning.

▶ **TASK 14**

Now consider your own beliefs and expectations about what happens in language-learning classrooms.

1 How do you think learners should participate? Should they work under the strong direction of the teacher or should they have some autonomy?

2 Do you think that learning a language is essentially
   – learning the grammar and pronunciation, or
   – learning the skills of reading, writing, speaking, and listening in the foreign language, or
   – learning to communicate in the language?

3 Is the teacher the final arbiter of correct and incorrect forms in the language classroom?

4 Do you think that the language classroom differs fundamentally in character from the science or maths or geography classroom? If so, in what ways?

Your answers here will reflect your attitudes towards and beliefs about classroom language learning. Your answers to 1 will have a direct influence on classroom behaviour. Your answers to 2 will have an indirect effect through the choice of learning content and materials. What do you think the effects of 3 and 4 will be? Direct or indirect?

Personality

Our personality fundamentally affects how we react under different circumstances. Many psychologists believe that our personalities are stable and constant, so that we are the same basic person whether we are in the role of teacher, learner, father, or son.

However, some individuals tend to be attracted by certain roles which they hope will satisfy their personal needs, such as a desire for power or caring for others. A further consideration is that the role itself may modify our personality so much that we behave 'out of context'. An example of this is the experienced teacher behaving like a teacher towards his nearest and dearest at home.

Another view is that our personalities are shaped only by experiences, in much the same way as attitudes are formed.

Consider the following questions:

> Which do you think is the best explanation of personality; that it is basically fixed, or that it develops and changes?
> What is the significance of personality for both teacher and learner? Do you think that only certain types of personality make ideal teachers and learners?
> What do you think of the view that we exhibit different aspects of our personalities in different social situations?

A typical description of personality types might include the following. *They are all tendencies, rather than absolute cut-and-dried descriptions*:

> Authoritarian: shows tendency for liking authority and exercising power
>
> Affiliative: shows tendency for preferring to form close relationships with others
>
> Conformist: shows tendency for wanting to think and act as others do
>
> Aggressive: shows tendency towards aggressive behaviour in order to achieve aims
>
> Co-operative: shows tendency to work closely with others in performing tasks
>
> Achieving: shows tendency towards wanting to achieve status, power, success.

In group activities like classroom language learning, it is likely that one's personality will affect the role one takes. It will also affect the interpretation of that role. The role, too, may also affect the individual's personality and thus give rise to certain modes of behaviour.

Teachers can, for example, choose *affiliative* behaviour. They may consciously attempt to create a warm, supportive classroom atmosphere with close relations between all participants.

On the other hand, they may attempt to control the thoughts, attitudes, and emotions of the learners. This is *dominant* behaviour.

Although teachers may tend to one or the other of these extremes, this is not only the result of personality. Other important influences include people like parents, colleagues, and administrators and above all the learners themselves. Social norms inside and outside the classroom may force the teacher into dominant behaviour. Attempts at affiliative behaviour in such circumstances would probably meet with severe resistance and create precisely the opposite effect.

A personality profile based on the sorts of criteria drawn up above may give indications of the likely success or problems an individual may face when engaged in a group activity in a particular role.

Think about this:

> Given the descriptions above, which tendencies do you think would make for successful teaching behaviour and which for successful learner behaviour in your culture?
> Would any particular combinations be particularly favourable?

In social situations, role behaviour tends to polarize around three axes:

> extroversion/introversion—outward or inward-looking behaviour;
> dominance/submission—behaviour directed towards control or being controlled;
> poise/social anxiety—confident or anxious behaviour.

Consider the following questions:

> Which of the above behaviours do you think are most appropriate for teachers on the one hand and learners on the other?
>
> Do you think that it is likely that teachers and learners will behave in ways contrary to your expectations expressed above? If so, in what sorts of situation (e.g. when learners are confronted with new language or pronunciation patterns that they find difficulty with)?
>
> How far do you believe that one's language is very much a part of one's personality and that learning a foreign language is very much akin to developing a new personality?
>
> How might the process of learning a new language and developing new personality traits lead to difficulties for learners in interpreting their role?

▶ ## TASK 15

You are going to draw up 'ideal' personality profiles for a set of roles.

> Doctor (D)   Learner (L)
> Lawyer (La)   Teacher (T)
> Librarian (Li)   Nurse (N)

Place the letter corresponding to each role in the appropriate place in each example depending on the tendency that you think is best for the particular role. For example, you may think that it is important that a doctor is relatively authoritarian, otherwise his patients may not do what he advises them to do. You would put 'D' in the place indicated below. You may consider that a librarian's role is best filled by an introvert. Accordingly, put 'Li' in the place as indicated. If you think there is no clear indication one way or another, put the letter in the middle of the line.

```
authoritarian   D                              democratic
    affiliative   _____   individualistic
    conformist    _____   non-conformist
    aggressive    _____   gentle
  co-operative    _____   competitive
     achieving    _____   non-achieving
     dominant     _____   submissive
     extrovert    _____Li_____  introvert
       poised     _____   anxious
    sensitive     _____   insensitive
```

Which of the roles you have looked at make the most powerful personal demands on the individuals who occupy them? What special social skills are required of these roles, e.g. convincing people that a course of action is in their best interests?

Motivation

We are interested in what motivates us to adopt certain roles. We are also interested in what motivates or demotivates us when we find ourselves in roles which are imposed upon us. By considering the factors which make us feel positive or negative about doing a certain task we can also gain an understanding of what it is that motivates teachers and learners.

It seems reasonable that if we choose a certain role, we are going to feel very positive about doing what is required to fulfil it. Initially, at least. But with those roles that are either imposed upon us or somehow acquired we may well feel differently. In order to find out why, we must examine the factors that appear to influence motivation.

Personal factors

Personality: We remarked in the previous section that certain personality types are attracted to certain roles. These personalities expect that the role will enable them to fulfil their needs. For example, a conformist type may be more likely to be attracted to a role where little initiative or leadership is needed.

Beliefs and attitudes: Positive beliefs about a role or the role expectations may also draw an individual towards the role. We may feel that we are able to 'do good' in a certain role. Do you think that this type of attitude is appropriate for a teacher?

The basic question that an individual might ask himself is, 'What can I expect from this role?' In finding an answer to that question, the individual has, among other things, to consider his own personal beliefs and attitudes, even his personality. People unsure of what sort of career they wish to pursue sometimes go for vocational guidance. Part of the vocational guidance procedure is to explore the individual's beliefs, attitudes, and values and to establish what sort of person he is and whether he will be happy and productive in the role he has chosen.

Personal needs: We can also look at motivation from the point of view of an individual's personal needs. Following the work of the American psychologist, Abraham Maslow (1968), we can see every individual as having a hierarchy of personal or human needs (see Figure 3).

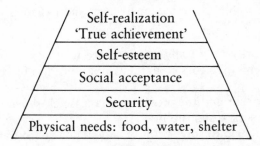

Figure 3. Maslow's hierarchy of needs

If we see human beings as having a course of development up the hierarchy, we can glimpse motivation of a deeper and more personal kind at work. Maslow's work was done with *happy and fulfilled* people who had achieved a great deal in their lives and had reached the top of the pyramid. He argued that people could not achieve the highest state of personal development unless the 'lower order needs' had been fulfilled. He assumed that people were naturally motivated to achieve higher order needs.

> Do people in your society see needs in the same way as Maslow? What relevance does this scheme have for learners of a second or foreign language? Where does such an undertaking fit in on the hierarchy?
> How far are you, personally, committed to such a view of motivation?

Some further points for you to dwell on:

> Is learning in itself a means of personal progress?
> Are our jobs a means of achieving personal happiness?
> Can we help others to achieve non-material gains in their lives?

Another American psychologist, McGregor (1960), investigating how people in different organizations achieve goals or have difficulties in achieving goals, would answer the third question in this way:

> We can only help others do well if we believe that they are capable of doing well.

McGregor proposed two broad types of organization, Theory X and Theory Y.

Theory X organizations believe:

1 The average human being has an inherent dislike of work and will avoid it if he can.
2 People must be coerced, controlled, directed, or threatened with punishment to get them to contribute to the achievement of organizational objectives.
3 The average human prefers to be directed, wishes to avoid responsibility, has little ambition, and wants security more than anything else.

Theory Y organizations believe:

1 People enjoy work as naturally as play or rest.
2 If people are committed to a goal, they do not need to be coerced into action.
3 People need rewards and the most important is self-satisfaction.
4 People learn to seek responsibility.
5 Most people can help to solve problems in an imaginative and creative manner.
6 Intellectual potential is only partially utilized.

Both of these views of human nature and motivation are important in our consideration of teacher and learner roles.

Think about the following:

How important is it for learners to set themselves personal goals?
Are educational beliefs in your society of the Theory X or Theory Y variety?
What are the implications for the distribution of power in the classroom of the Theory Y view?
Do you believe that the best way to become responsible is to learn to take responsibility? Does this also apply to one's own learning?
Language learning is a problem-solving activity—do you agree?

Types of motivation

Why do people spend so much time and effort learning foreign languages? Are there any other factors apart from the personal factors we have already considered which have an influence?

Major studies have found that people are either *integratively* or *instrumentally* motivated towards learning a foreign language. This distinction is based on extensive study of:

Cultural beliefs about learning a second language: It is believed that these will influence the positive or negative motivation individuals have towards learning a language. If the culture values the activity then it is likely that there will be a positive motivation. This has been termed 'integrative' motivation.

Attitudes: If the society holds positive attitudes towards the L2 group, it is believed that *integrative* motivation will drive learners towards the acquisition of the language, regardless of the possible loss of cultural identity this might cause. The studies have concluded that *instrumental* factors such as fear of failure, desire to do well at school or future job requirements do not have the power to maintain the long-term effort of learning a foreign language of the *integrative* factors such as a low degree of ethnocentrism, a desire to 'be like others', and a love of other cultures and ways of life.

More recent studies (cf. Giles and Byrne 1982) have cast doubt on the instrumental/integrative distinction but still acknowledge the importance of positive attitudes towards the L2 community as well as the instrumental aspect of motivation.

All of this has serious implications for the role expectations of learners. If there is high motivation, either integrative or instrumental, among a group of learners, it is likely that they will seek:

1 to *synchronize* their roles with their teacher's role;
2 to *co-operate* in the arduous task of learning the language in question in order to maximize the benefits they receive with higher status, better jobs, or a sense of personal achievement from mastering the language.

▶ TASK 16

Study the seven statements which follow and decide whether:

1 they contain elements of instrumental motivation and integrative motivation;
2 they are attitudes or beliefs which are widely adhered to in your society;
3 they illustrate any of the values that may be held in common by teachers and learners in your society.

  a. Learning a language is an interesting task.
  b. If we speak a second language it will be easier to get a job.
  c. Learning a language is good mental discipline.
  d. It is both interesting and desirable to learn about other people's cultures.
  e. Acquiring foreign languages is both desirable and necessary for civilized existence.
  f. Learning foreign languages gives you the chance to travel.
  g. Speaking a foreign language shows that a person is educated.

4 What connections do you see between the personal types of motivation referred to in the earlier part of this section and factors such as instrumentality and integration? For example, do you think the satisfaction of personal needs is an instrumental or integrative process or contains elements of both?

Can motivation be increased?
Faced with a group of learners with apparently low motivation what, if anything, can a teacher do to increase its level?

First, what are the symptoms of low motivation? Learners may exhibit a negative attitude to the subject you are teaching. They may not participate very keenly in class or avoid doing assignments. Attendance may fall off and the learners who continue coming to class may be disruptive. These are not necessarily symptoms only of low motivation. There could be other, deeper causes, such as an alienation from school, for this type of behaviour.

It is imperative, therefore, that we try to diagnose the causes of the problem before it negates all our efforts in the classroom. We can achieve nothing without the co-operation of the learners. The learners can achieve little without the co-operation of their teachers, too.

We shall examine this and related questions in more detail in Section Two. As a prelude to the discussion, think about the following questions:

Can motivation be increased by the choice of appropriate tasks?
How important is the teacher's personality as a motivating force?
Can we change people's attitudes to learning?
Are some school 'subjects' intrinsically more interesting than others?
Do some learners have a better aptitude for certain areas of study and are they therefore better motivated in these areas?
Do certain patterns of organization in the classroom give rise to better motivation?
Does responsibility lead to higher motivation?
Does choice of learning materials and modes of learning by the learner lead to higher motivation?

Goals
Social behaviour is goal-directed. People have differing personal and instrumental motivations for their actions. From the simple act of saying 'good morning' as we pass an acquaintance in the street to the higher planes of self-actualization, there are goals implicit in our actions.

We may, in certain roles, have to subscribe to goals not of our own choice. There may be institutional goals which conflict with our attitudes or beliefs, for example. In other roles, we may find the perfect vehicles for the achievement of our personal and instrumental goals. The way in which we interpret and realize goals is part of role-behaviour.

Successful fulfilment of a role may be the result of what the social psychologist Michael Argyle (1969) calls 'skilled performance'. Doing certain jobs or taking roles entail various goals. These are, variously:

1 conveying knowledge, information, or understanding
2 obtaining information from or about an individual
3 changing attitudes, behaviour, or beliefs

4 changing the emotional state of another individual
5 working at a co-operative task
6 changing the personality of another individual
7 supervising the activities of another individual
8 supervising and co-ordinating the activities of a group.

Any role may encompass one or more of these goals for its successful realization. However, there is sure to be a *primary goal* attached to the role. Other goal-directed behaviour is *subsidiary* and supportive of the primary goal.

For example, telling a joke may have the primary aim of changing another's emotional state. The joke itself may come about during an activity such as supervising. The subsidiary aim may be to 'jolly the person along', to relax them. As a by-product, the individual's reaction to the joke may give hints about his or her attitudes and beliefs.

A skilled social performer will be aware of his influence through successful role behaviour—behaviour which conforms to expectations, so that roles fit, and goals are achieved.

▶ TASK 17

1 Examine again the list of goals outlined above.
Which seem to be predominantly interpersonal?
Which seem to be predominantly task-oriented?

2 Match up the goals to the following activities:

selling somebody a car
bringing up children
working on a factory production line
nursing a sick person
interviewing a candidate for a job
chairing a committee
dealing with a hostile person
giving a lecture

3 Which of the goals above is the most important for a teacher and which for a learner?

4 In your role as a teacher, can you think of activities which realize any of the other goals? Make a list of these.

2.2 Task-related factors

What is a task?

Clearly a task is more than just an activity, more than 'doing something'. In the context of classroom language learning, there are various tasks which teachers and learners have to perform. They must be seen as goal-directed, both in the short term, during a lesson, and over the long term, during a course.

Think about the tasks you have attempted so far in this book:

Have they involved thinking?
Have they involved feelings, attitudes, beliefs?
Have they involved making judgements?
Have you attempted the tasks alone or with the assistance and company of friends and colleagues? Which has proved more valuable?

There are two main elements of a task – the *cognitive*, or 'thinking' aspect, and the *affective*, or 'feeling' aspect. When groups work on a task, they take up roles which bring together the cognitive and affective aspects of the task.

Any learning task involves the learning group in two ways:

1 task-related activity or *interactivity*
2 interpersonal activity or *interpersonality*.

Interactivity

The nature of the learning activity and the way in which it is managed by the learning group will give rise to differing levels of learner and teacher involvement. Activities can thus be placed between the extremes of learner interaction with the teaching materials or the teacher, and maximum learner involvement in group activity.

Interpersonality

The amount and type of subject or topic-oriented material in any learning activity will enable us to see whether or not the task is *instrumental* – a means of acquiring facts or *interpersonal* – dominated by learners' own contributions. This can be summarized diagrammatically:

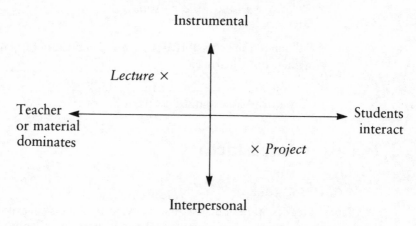

Figure 4 (after McLeish 1973)

What do teachers do to get learners to learn?

A task is goal-directed in the sense of bringing about changes in behaviour or knowledge. Within any activity, there may be a number of tasks to perform, each with its own definite goal. For example, think about the 'reading lesson' as an activity, within which a number of tasks may be performed by both teachers and learners, such as organizing the classroom layout, presenting the texts in whatever way is deemed appropriate, doing 'exercises' on the texts and so on.

▶ TASK 18

Can you divide the list of teaching and learning tasks which follow into two groups – those with a high cognitive element and those with a high affective element? Which do you think are very interactive (dominated by teacher or materials) and which do you see as interpersonal (involving learners' personal contributions)?

> organizing pair work
> learning twenty items of vocabulary
> doing a structure drill
> evaluating the success of a group activity
> marking compositions
> taking part in a role play
> taking part in an open discussion of a topic
> choosing a composition topic
> doing a pronunciation drill
> working on a listening text in the language laboratory
> explaining a grammar point

Do you have any reservations about the categories you have made up? If so, why? Did you find yourself thinking that the task could have been in either category, depending on the way in which it was handled by either teacher or learner? For example, a role play could have both a high cognitive and a high affective load in that the language required is difficult *and* the situation involves a certain amount of emotional commitment from the participants.

Cognitively, a task may be 'difficult' or 'complex' – this may be intrinsic to the task or related to the intelligence or aptitude of the individual performing the task.

A task can also be 'difficult' because an individual has a negative attitude towards it, or its contents, or the people with whom he is doing the task. Motivation can be increased by success, of course, encouraging one to attempt further tasks.

A task can also be 'difficult' because of the level of affective involvement it entails. The task may be too demanding of a learner's emotional commitment. Combined with a high cognitive involvement, it can make the task all but impossible to do.

Solitary or co-operative?

We are also interested in the influence of tasks on group and therefore role behaviour.

> Is teaching a solitary or co-operative task?
> Is learning a language a solitary or co-operative task?
> Does teaching imply certain tasks and certain goals?

To think about:

> What aspects of a teacher's role are solitary?
> What aspects of a teacher's role are co-operative?
> What happens when groups work on tasks?

Answers to all the questions so far raised may be found in an examination of the work of experimental psychologists on group processes.

2.3 Group processes

How do groups evolve?

A classic study of problem-solving groups (Tuckman 1965, quoted in Argyle 1969) established that a small group went through four stages from its formation. This has great relevance for our study of the classroom and also the use of group study/activities during teaching. The study also links the social processes of the group with the task the group undertakes.

Stage 1 Forming: In the group, there is some anxiety. There is a great deal of dependence on the leader (the teacher) and a great deal of behaviour directed towards finding out the nature of the situation and also what behaviour is acceptable.

At the same time, group members attempt to find out what the task is, what the rules are for carrying out the task and the methods that are appropriate.

Stage 2 Storming: There is now conflict between sub-groups and also rebellion against the leader. Opinions are extreme and there is resistance to group control. Role relations are not agreed upon. All of this behaviour is a resistance to the demands of the task.

Stage 3 Norming: The group develops cohesion: norms of behaviour emerge and participants begin to accept group control. Conflicts are forgotten and members begin to support each other. At this stage co-operation is the rule and there is open exchange of views and feelings about the task and each other.

Stage 4 Performing: All individuals' problems are resolved and there is a great deal of interpersonal activity. Members' roles in the group now lose their rigidity and become more functional. At this stage solutions to the problems of the task are found and all efforts are devoted to completing the task.

▶ TASK 19

Study the types of behaviour below and decide whether they are examples of Stage 1, 2, 3, or 4 in the formation of a group. Enter the stage number in the column to the left of the statements.

Stage	Types of behaviour
	Member encourages others to keep working
	Member refuses to accept majority decision
	Member willingly agrees to change role in group
	Members brainstorm ideas about task
	Leader accepts group's decision
	Members converge on task solution
	Member refuses to divulge personal feelings
	Members agree to take a break from work
	Member takes on a new role which is accepted by the group

Note how, in the experimental work, there was a strong tendency to solve social or interpersonal problems before getting down to the task itself.

This may strike you as familiar. Perhaps we have seen a class we teach develop in this way? Perhaps we teach a class stuck in Stage 2? There are differences between this pattern and the teacher-led group, though. And we must keep these in mind.

1 In the experimental work, the leader was 'elected' by the group. The power relationship was referent.
2 All members had equal or roughly equal status. There was relatively low social distance between members.
3 The task was perceived to be central to the group's existence.
4 Motivation was generally very high among members and behaviour was overtly goal-oriented in a positive manner.

One of the conclusions drawn from the research was that when learners are involved in setting group goals, their affective involvement and motivation were noticeably higher. The learners not only perform better but they behave better, too. This contrasts with the customary idea that it is the teacher who sets the goals in a learning group, or carries out the plan of a centrally-decided curriculum.

Norms and expectations

Groups tend towards normative behaviour, once conflicts between individual members have been resolved. We must beware of seeing this tendency towards 'normal' behaviour as a once and for all process though. It is more realistic to see the learning group developing over time as the personalities of the individuals develop. The type of leadership that emerges, the types of activity performed and the cumulative effect of these also play a part. Participants' goals may change over time, too, and set up new expectations.

Norms are likely to develop about:

the level of informality or formality of the group
the type of control preferred, whether internally or externally imposed
the types of learning activity preferred by the group
how much revelation of one's personal feelings is permitted or played down.

All of these contribute to the participants' expectations.

▶   TASK 20

Think about your own learning group(s) and consider the norms that they display.

1   What level of formality is expected?
2   What sort of control is preferred?
3   What sorts of learning activity are preferred?
4   How much are personal feelings revealed about topics in the classroom?
5   Do you think this set of norms applies to your culture in general?

Communication patterns in groups

We have seen the stages that groups appear to go through as they develop. What sort of communication patterns develop at the 'norming' and 'performing' stages?

Research into the communication patterns of small groups under laboratory conditions (Leavitt 1951) revealed the following broad patterns:

1 Multi-channel

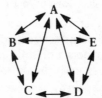

Figure 5

This pattern, with 100% connectivity between the group members, is very satisfactory from a personal point of view, since every member has the opportunity to communicate with all the other members. Communication is unrestricted and there is no leader in the sense of a dominant member of the group. The time taken to solve problems was significantly longer than for the other patterns, but group members reported a better personal rapport than the others.

2 Circle

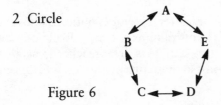

Figure 6

This pattern has only 50% connectivity between its members. Further, members only have direct communication with those who are immediately adjacent to them. Thus **A** has direct links with only **E** and **B**. Problem-solving efficiency was, however, distinctly quicker, especially if information was channelled to one member.

3 The 'Y'

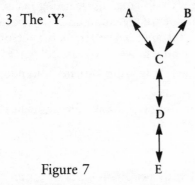

Figure 7

This pattern made fewer errors in problem-solving tasks, since information flowed through member **C**. The group was slower than the circle, however.

4 The 'wheel'

Like the **Y** group, this pattern has only 40% connectivity and was very efficient at problem-solving because of **A**'s central position and role of information processor. However, as the task becomes more complex, **A** tends to become overburdened and loses efficiency.

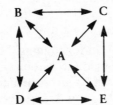

Figure 8

These formal organizational *networks* have a great deal of significance for the organization of classroom activities. For example, if one sees the teacher as occupying a position similar to that of **A** in the wheel network, one can imagine the heavy responsibility that he has for the success of the activity.

▶ TASK 21

1 Referring to the communication networks outlined above, try to match them with what you think is the most likely outcome of certain language learning activities. The teacher is at all times assumed to be taking part in the activity either as director or equal participant.

open-ended discussion
structure drill
explanation of the meaning of a vocabulary item
oral feedback on a set of comprehension questions
simulation

2 What do you think are the implications for organizing the class into small working groups to do language learning tasks? What are the factors that will influence the communication patterns in the groups you set up? For instance, do you think the personalities of the individual group members will have an influence?

3 Will the type of task have a bearing on the communication pattern that emerges?

4 Do you think the subject matter will have any influence?

2.4 Topics

In any social interaction, we deal with two main types of topic:

1 the way the social interaction proceeds – *procedural topics*
2 'subject matter' or 'knowledge' – *content topics*.

Procedural topics

In the 'forming' and 'storming' stages of a group's existence, a large number of topics will be procedural.
These may include:

1 the right of an individual to change topic
2 the right of an individual to introduce a topic
3 the right of an individual to close a topic.

If the group leader takes sole rights for running the group and thus control of the procedure, then he controls the topics. In the storming stage, members may dispute this claim. Only when the procedural rules for running the group are established can this source of conflict be removed.

There is a clear link with role expectations here: if we expect one group member to be in control of topics (for example, a chairman), this is part of the role behaviour. If the leader does not control the procedure, a free-for-all may result. Our expectations will have been disappointed. We, too, join the free-for-all: out of frustration rather than any other cause.

In classrooms, there may also be similar processes at work. Teachers often decide which learner is to answer a question by nominating individuals by name. Some teachers prefer to let their class 'bid' to give the answers, picking seemingly at random an individual from the group. It is clear that there are conventions for topic control in classrooms—these derive partly from the teacher's authority and partly from the social conventions operating in any particular place. Sometimes, the procedures for letting people hold the floor may differ from the world outside the classroom and conflict can result. In classrooms, it is important to 'know the rules' for who can speak at any given moment. These systems of exchange are crucial to our understanding of classroom behaviour.

▶ TASK 22

In your society, are there 'rules' for conducting various group activities, e.g. public meetings, etc.?
If so, can you state some of them?

Example: An individual may not speak unless he has been given the floor by the group leader.

Are these 'rules' replicated in the classroom?

Knowledge

Managing knowledge
The second type of topic may also be understood as the 'subject' people are discussing. This is:

1 related to the task we are engaged in;
2 related to the behaviour expected of us in our various roles;
3 related to what we, as individuals, actually *know*.

The combinations of teacher behaviour, learner behaviour, and learning materials produce different ways of managing knowledge.

Walker and Adelman (1975) differentiate between three ways in which teachers manage knowledge. These depend on the level of focus on the content and the role of the learner. If a learner's role is defined closely, it is the teacher who has control over the knowledge; a low-definition learner role gives the learner more flexibility. In this relationship, the teacher is a guide rather than an instructor.

Focusing: The content of the lesson is paramount and the teaching/learning process revolves around evaluation of the knowledge possessed by the learners. The teacher is in a position of dominance and controls the exchanges of information.

Cook's Tour: The content is again the focus of the lesson, but this style of management is on the surface, more open-ended than the focusing style. The lesson is based on the achievement of content goals, but the teacher sets more open-ended tasks for the achievement of these goals. Correct answers are discovered rather than directly elicited.

Freewheeling: Lessons are extremely discursive, and to an outsider may seem unstructured and fragmented. There is a free flow of talk between teachers and learners and many different subjects may be covered in one 'tour'. The outcome is highly unpredictable.

The management of knowledge can be summarized diagrammatically in this way:

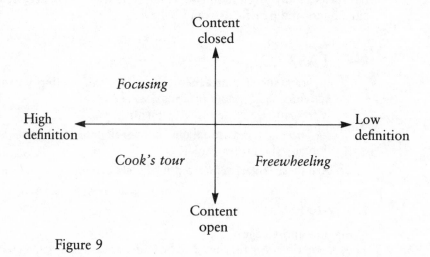

Figure 9

▶ TASK 23

What do you think would be the outcome of the following language learning tasks, using the Walker and Adelman categorization?

1 Discussion on 'The Effects of Youth Unemployment' as a prelude to writing an essay with a similar title.
2 Structure drill with a substitution table on the blackboard.
3 Discussion on the possible meanings of a new item of vocabulary.
4 Role play: learners in pairs—one is a doctor, the other a patient. The patient is complaining about a cold and the doctor is sympathizing. Expressions of complaint and sympathy are given.
5 Oral composition based on a story told to the class by the teacher.

What sorts of knowledge are involved in each of the activities: knowledge of language? social situations? knowledge of the world?

How closely can the teacher control the knowledge in each of the activities?

Does the learner have any choices in the type of knowledge that can be used in each activity?

Unequal shares

Knowledge is rarely shared out equally among us. The unequal distribution here is similar to the unequal distribution of power. A large proportion of communicative activity is concerned with transmitting and receiving knowledge; or reducing our relative ignorance about the world, events we have not experienced, or our more intimate knowledge of the feelings of others.

▶ **TASK 24**

We expect individuals in certain roles to have extensive knowledge about certain subjects.

Examine the list below and tick those types of knowledge that you expect a language teacher to possess:

> the grammatical and phonological systems of the language
> a wide range of subjects such as science, history and religion
> how people interact socially
> psychological processes
> theories of learning
> contemporary world affairs
> young people's interests
> different modes of classroom activity
> a variety of teaching techniques
> literature in the language being taught
> a large active vocabulary

Of the types of knowledge you have considered, which do you think are the most important for the teacher?

How do you think your choice manifests itself in the goals you set for your learners?

What sort of assumptions are you making here about language teaching in terms of its content and the way you go about it?

Do you think your learners have similar expectations to yours as to the types of knowledge you should possess?

In the role of teacher, we may discern two related types of knowledge being utilized. First, the procedural knowledge of how to organize and set up classroom activities, and the second, 'subject' knowledge of the language being taught.

The two are linked through teaching methods and techniques which are aimed at bringing about learning.

Teaching and learning are goal-directed activities, with learning the focal goal: both teachers and learners want to see that language is being learnt. However, the two parties may disagree as to the way in which this is best achieved. A typical example is of the learner who perceives his goal as the learning of the grammar of the language and the teacher who sees the goal as the learning of a system of communicative functions.

Such a conflict of belief about the nature of language itself is more common than many teachers would like to admit. Implicit in both positions is the role of teacher and learner: teacher as provider of information and learner as receptacle for this information. This crude statement of the position masks many other 'hidden' roles which we examine in more detail in Section Two.

Group processes: review

The act of working together with a group of people all trying to solve the same problem as we would be in the language classroom is very likely to change our behaviour.

Affecting ourselves
1 Our attitudes and beliefs can be modified.
2 We can increase our store of knowledge about the topic we are dealing with.
3 We may come to understand more about the way we work in the company of others.
4 We may be forced to look afresh at our own personalities—our self-awareness may have increased.
5 We will directly experience role-behaviour, although we may be unaware of the fact.

Affecting the group
1 We will form relationships with others in the group. We will find 'things in common' with others in the group and may share our beliefs and perceptions with others.
2 We will all become aware of how people behave in different roles, how these roles may be interpreted in a way contrary to our prior expectations.

Performing
The process of doing the task will directly link our personal goals and the inbuilt or 'hidden' goals of the task.

Interlocking roles
In group activities, our roles *interlock*. A role is only fulfilled if we agree that the individual and the role 'fit' and that the role 'fits' with our role.

We synchronize our behaviour in co-operative ventures and receive positive or negative reactions from the others in the social encounter in question. Thus we tend to modify our role behaviour towards group norms or what the group feels the appropriate behaviour is. *Role behaviour results from interaction with others.*

Interpretation

Although we may wish to interpret our role in a certain way, we can only carry through the interpretation if we are allowed to by the others in the group. The only way in which we can do this otherwise is to impose any power we may have on the other group members. It may happen that our behaviour may be misinterpreted—conflict will arise, conflict which can only be resolved by modification of behaviour or a reinterpretation by our fellows of our behaviour. All role behaviour can lead to conflict if roles do not interlock.

▶ TASK 25

Examine the quote which follows:

> Two people must agree on the role-relations between them—if one is a teacher, the other must be a pupil.
> (Argyle 1969: 200)

Can you list the occasions when teachers and learners may not agree on the role relations between them?

Consider any of the factors which influence our interpretation of a role.

2.5 Teacher and learner roles: summary

Let us briefly summarize what influences the role relations between teachers and learners in order to come to some preliminary conclusions.

Interpersonal factors

Status and position: Teachers and learners are accorded social status depending on what we value in their performances. The relative positions are usually fixed, although types of teaching and learning situation differ a great deal.

A power relationship exists between teachers and learners in which power is not shared equally. This fact, combined with perceptions of status, gives rise to social distance.

Attitudes, beliefs: While teachers have a set of professional attitudes, personal attitudes and beliefs are likely to differ considerably between teachers and learners. The attitudes may be towards teaching and learning, the 'content' of learning or each other as people.

Personality: All individuals bring their personalities into social encounters. Indeed, social life is a major factor in shaping personality. In the intimacy of the teaching/learning situation, it is extremely likely that personalities will be modified. An additional complication arises in the situation where learners are trying to cope with a foreign language. The internalization of the new language may bring about changes in the personality of the learner.

Motivation: Teachers have motivations for teaching and learners for learning, both instrumental and integrative. Teachers and learners also have deeper, more personal goals. These are linked to

Task-related factors

Goals: Every task has goals or solutions. Individuals' personal goals may be activated by tasks. Teachers and learners are engaged in an activity that is very dependent on goals.

Tasks: As well as the affective, or 'personal', side of tasks, there is the cognitive, or mental, side. During group tasks in the classroom, there is an interplay between the two aspects.

Topics: Tasks themselves usually have 'subject matter' or skills inherent to them. While doing a task, an individual may also have to decide on the procedure for doing the tasks. A great deal of classroom activity is devoted to topics, both procedural and 'subject'.

▶ TASK 26

1 Study each of the role-determining factors again and then rank them in order of importance for both teachers and learners. Your ordering will give you some insight into the priorities of the teaching/learning environment where you work at present.

2 How do you think your society rates each factor? Do you think you have the same priorities as the general public in your country?

3 Make a list of questions on the roles of teachers and learners that *you* would like to find the answers to.

Refer back to any part of Section One which intrigues you or you find difficulty in grasping.

Try to phrase your questions using the terminology of Section One.

While you are doing this task, consider the following:

Which do you think are the important features of teacher and learner role you need more information on?

Which features of teacher and learner role do you think would be interesting to investigate, particularly in your own school or society/culture?

In what ways do you think teacher and learner role will influence classroom activities? What will the activities demand of the teacher and the learner? How far and in what ways do you think classroom language learning is a social activity?

Now refer back to your notes from the introduction and tasks in this section.

Have your ideas changed as a result of reading the section?

Have you come across concepts or aspects of the teaching/learning situation that you were previously unaware of?

Teacher and learner roles in the classroom

In this section, our aims are threefold:

1 to see how the concepts discussed in Section One are realized in action in the classroom
2 to see how teacher and learner roles are seen in various teachers' handbooks and teachers' guides to published materials
3 to see what teaching materials predetermine and/or imply for teacher and learner roles.

In this section, you are free to follow whatever route you wish to take through the text. If you have already looked at Section One, you may well have an agenda of topics you wish to explore or find out more about. Alternatively, you may want to work through the section sequentially.

The section is in two main parts. The first deals with issues relating to the teacher's role; the second deals with issues concerning the learner's role.

Before embarking on this section, pause to consider this characterization of the teacher's role by Gerald Dykstra:

> ... near automatons who stand up, call roll, talk a lot, give cues, ask simple content questions, check for comprehension, check for recall, keep records, discipline students, bestow grades and generally carry on with clerical tasks far below what their own level of ability might be.
> (Dykstra 1978: 4)

Is this how you would characterize yourself as a teacher? What rings true in Dykstra's comments? What is very definitely untrue in your particular case?

3 Teaching tasks and teaching strategies

In Section One, we looked at the various factors which influence the way teachers interpret their roles in the classroom. Our aim in this section is to find out what teachers and learners actually do in the classroom; our focus is on teacher and learner role behaviour. We must continually bear in mind the close relationship between the teacher and the learner roles.

This interdependence is well illustrated by the quotation which follows.

> . . . in general it might be said that teachers would be expected as a minimum part of their role to have adequate knowledge of their subject matter, to know something of how children learn and develop and to be able to devise appropriate learning/teaching experiences in the light of these two considerations. Pupils would be expected as a minimum part of their role to be interested in being learners, to develop the skills of listening to a teacher's exposition of a topic and to acquire the skills of reading about and understanding subject matter as well as developing some skill with numbers.
> (Cortis 1977: 20)

► TASK 27

Study the extract above and comment on the following ideas:

1 The teacher's most important task is to impart knowledge.
2 The learner's most important task is to listen.
3 The author ignores the conditions under which learning takes place.
4 The author appears to be interested more in the instructional task of teaching than the interpersonal side of teaching.
5 The author assumes that teachers have full authority and power in the classroom.

Now consider the extract which follows and compare it with Cortis:

> The concept of the teacher as 'instructor' is [. . .] inadequate to describe his overall function. In a broad sense, he is a 'facilitator of learning', and may need to perform in a variety of roles, separately or simultaneously.
> (Littlewood 1981: 92)

Essentially, teachers have two major roles in the classroom:

1 to create the conditions under which learning can take place: the social side of teaching;

2 to impart, by a variety of means, knowledge to their learners: the task-oriented side of teaching.

Figure 10

The first we shall term the 'enabling' or *management* function and the second the *instructional* function. They complement each other; the latter would be more or less impossible without the former. In practice, it is very difficult to separate the two and often one act in the classroom can perform both functions simultaneously.

What does the management of the learning group entail?

3.1 Teaching style

A teacher's *style* is the collection of the many attitudes and behaviours he employs to create the best possible conditions under which learning can take place. The teacher's primary role when setting up learning activities is *managerial*.

▶ TASK 28

Reading the list of management behaviours that follows. Which do you think are the most appropriate for creating the best conditions for learning to take place?

Giving learners plenty of encouragement for their efforts.
Establishing a position of dominance over the learners.
Ignoring disruptive behaviour and praising appropriate behaviour.
Giving pupils responsibility for their learning.
Learning the names of the learners quickly.
Keeping registers up to date.
Being warm, friendly and open with the learners.
Establishing a routine of working patterns.

Threatening learners who misbehave with punishment.
Setting learning tasks which are completed in total silence.
Which ones require the imposition of the teacher's power for their success?
Which ones involve a lowering of social distance?
Which of these behaviours are task-oriented?
Are any likely to influence the motivation of the learners? If so, in what ways?

You might have concluded that any of the management behaviours is appropriate, *depending on the circumstances.*
What are your circumstances?

What do your learners expect? What do their parents expect (if this applies)? What does the administration of your institution want of its teachers?

Motivation

A primary function of teachers' management role is to motivate the learners who are demotivated and to nurture those who are already well motivated to the task of learning a foreign language. There are several ways in which teachers can achieve this.

1 Adopting a positive attitude towards the learners. For example, a certain language point may take the learners some time to absorb. Praise and encouragement for positive efforts by the learners will help to keep motivation up.

2 Giving pupils meaningful, relevant, and interesting tasks to do. We look at this more closely under *Learning activities* in Unit 4 below.

3 Maintaining discipline to the extent that a reasonable working atmosphere is established. This does not necessarily mean total silence, rather an atmosphere of calm and organization.

4 Being motivated and interested themselves. It is an inevitable outcome of any occupation that one becomes bored and uninterested from time to time. (If it is more frequent, then one has to consider leaving the occupation or seeking expert assistance!)

5 Involving the learners more actively in the classroom process in activities that demand inter-student communication and co-operative efforts on their part. Group work and simulations are two examples of such activities that are designed to achieve this effect.

6 Introducing learners to the concept of self-appraisal and self-evaluation through reports and discussions.

7 Giving positive feedback on written assignments.

8 Encouraging pride in achievement by allowing learners to display their work on the classroom walls and noticeboards.

▶   TASK 29

Which of these strategies seem familiar to you? Are there any that strike you as strange or potentially problematical?

Which of these strategies do you think would go farthest towards helping learners to achieve self respect and in effect to define their own role as learners more clearly? Do you think this might pose problems in your working environment?

Which of the strategies do you think involve risks? What sort of risks?

Control and discipline

Many views on teachers' managerial role derive from the assumption that teachers have a great deal of power over their learners. For example:

> If your students begin speaking in their own language without your permission, regard this as a danger signal.
> (Willis 1981: xiv)

Think about this:

> Do you find it strange or unusual that learners must ask permission to speak in their native language during a foreign language lesson? Are there any teaching/learning situations when this might not be appropriate?
> What sort of management role does the author imply for teachers?

We can have two differing perspectives on these questions. The first maintains that discipline imposed by the teacher is the basis of good management while a second hints at self-discipline.

There is a further strand of control that we must mention. Teachers also control the social and learning behaviour of their learners through the choice of activities and the ways in which they organize the learning group to do the activities.

Study the extract which follows in the light of what you have just read. What are the implications of the extract in terms of:

1 classroom discipline?
2 teacher control of behaviour and activities?
3 learner motivation?

Teacher 'overload' often entails learner 'underinvolvement' since teachers are doing work learners could more profitably do themselves.
(Allwright 1981: 10)

The implications may be that more responsibility needs to be given to the learner for deciding the agenda for learning and the best way to go about it. On the other hand, there may be specific teaching techniques and strategies that require strong central direction from the teacher in order to ensure their success. Choices have to be made between various modes of presenting learning activities. Gower and Walters put it this way:

. . . you need to subtly alter your role according to the activity without going to the extremes of dominating a class or leaving it without anything to do.
(Gower and Walters 1983: 7)

▶ **TASK 30**

Consider the extract which follows and discuss the questions which follow it.

The teacher plays the role of controller when he is totally in charge of the class. He controls not only what the students do, but when they speak and what language they use. Clearly the introduction of new language often involves the teacher in a controlling role, particularly at the accurate reproduction stage. We have suggested that there is good reason for conducting a short drilling session where the teacher indicates exactly what is to be said (or written) and who is going to say (or write) it . . .
(Harmer 1983: 201)

Do you think it is necessary for the teacher to be 'totally in charge of the class' at all times?

Why do you think the teacher needs to be in control at 'the accurate reproduction stage'?

Do you think it is realistic for learners to speak only when they are allowed to?

Do you think that the author is concerned with teaching or learning 'efficiency'?

Does the introduction of new language always involve the teacher in a controlling role? Can you think of any other ways in which new language can be introduced?

We may conclude that there are two types of control employed by teachers:

1 control of the social behaviour of the class
2 control over the class through the learning activity.

Often the two are inseparable, but we can see how the type of activity that the teaching/learning group is undertaking indicates the type of control teachers have over the learners.

What happens when discipline is poor? There are times when we encounter a teaching/learning situation that demands strong control and the imposition of discipline of one sort or another because the learners are badly behaved. What do you think are some of the causes of 'bad behaviour' (however you may wish to characterize it)?

Teachers tend to deal with such situations in several ways:

1 By attempting to socialize the learners – by prescribing certain learner roles and proscribing others. This can be achieved by coercion or by punishment.
2 The teacher can try to dominate the learners who break the rules. Open conflict can result.
3 The teacher can try negotiation: appeals, apologies, cajolery and flattery. Alternatively he can make promises or threats, try bribes and trade-offs.
4 The teacher can try to reduce social distance between himself and the learners. By fraternizing with the class the teacher also runs the risk of behaving counter to their expectations.
5 The teacher can set tasks which involve routine and control. Often the apparent threat of indiscipline can lead to such solutions. For example:
   setting activities with a definite time limit
   reciting from the textbook
   following the textbook to the letter
   making the learners copy notes
   using worksheets or workcards with definite and predictable outcomes.

► TASK 31

Consider the extracts which follow and comment on them with reference to the means of maintaining control outlined above.

1 Which strategy (or strategies) do you think the authors imply?

a. I began to see myself not as a leader but as an impresario giving new talent the opportunity to be born. This, then, I saw as the role of the teacher in the student-centred classroom. The teacher chooses and directs the music, but the resulting dance becomes one of the performer's own making.
(Salimbene 1981: 94)

b. The pupils behave largely as one many-headed participant, avoiding cross-conversations and acknowledging the authority of the teacher in their verbal behaviour.
(Sinclair and Brazil 1982: 3)

c. It appears that you must constantly get on to the children – in the sense that you deflate them; you've got to make them toe the line all the time, you cannot assume that they'll come in, and sit down and get on with the job.
(Gibson 1973: 72)

2 What do you think is the source of motivation in the classrooms decribed in the three extracts?

3 What sorts of underlying attitudes regarding the roles of teachers and learners are revealed in the extracts?

The fourth and fifth means of maintaining control differ from the first three in several ways. The learners' response to routine may be to accept the status quo – however, peace may have been won at the expense of meaningful learning. The problems are unlikely to go away.

What else can teachers do? An alternative is to disperse power among the learning group. Not completely, for that would be akin to handing over responsibility entirely to the learning group. Teachers may then be accused of failing to carry out their professional duties and fulfilling their obligations to the learners.

Organizing the learning group

There are several possible ways of organizing the learning group. Each one entails different types of relationships between teachers and learners and may be employed for a variety of different reasons. As well as implying different social relationships beween participants, the various organizational patterns also entail different types of product or contribution from the learners.

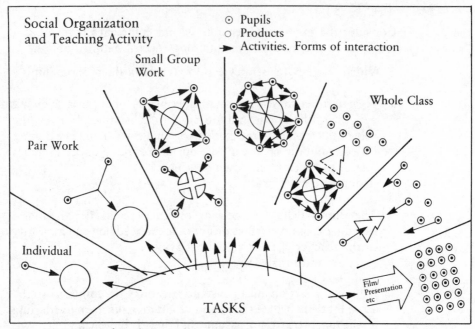

Figure 11   (Bundesarbeitsgemeinschaft Englisch an Gesamtschulen (B.A.G.)

2 Another commonly used organizational strategy is to put the class into small groups for certain tasks. For example the class can be divided into discussion groups of between two and eight students.

The solution of these tasks is the responsibility of the learners – although ultimate control is still in the hands of teachers. They can curtail activities at any time they choose.

Think about this:

How do you feel about dispersing power among small groups of learners?
Are there any local constraints (social or cultural) which would make this difficult?

3 Another way of varying the layout of the classroom is as follows:

It may be impossible to avoid having your students sitting in rows facing you. Even here, however, ensure that empty seats are only at the back and that everyone is grouped as near the front as possible. Ideally, everyone should be able to see everyone else, so that they can all participate in what is being said. Probably the best arrangement is to have everyone ranged round the wall, in a circle. You then get a large area in the middle which can be used for acting out, and there is a greater sense of community.
(Haycraft 1978: 15)

In Figure 12 below, where does the teacher sit?

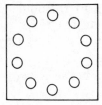

Figure 12

4 A further alternative is to arrange the learning group in a horseshoe, as illustrated in Figure 13 about which Langenheim observes (1980):

> The lessons involve the class working individually, in pairs, in groups, and the whole class together, so it is important to create a group feeling from the outset. As far as possible arrange your classroom to suit your activities. Don't let tables and desks create barriers, either use them if the situation requires it, or place them against the wall. Ideally, remember, we don't want a performance area; we want a space where anything can happen. Like this, for example:

Figure 13

5 A variety of seating arrangements may be employed during the course of a single lesson. For example:

> To say that reading is a silent and personal activity does not imply that it only lends itself to individual work. On the contrary, it is particularly interesting to encourage comparisons of a text which will lead to discussion and probably a need to refer back to the text to check. Here are possible steps:
>
> 1 Silent reading followed by an activity which each student does on his own.
> 2 The students now work in pairs, each one trying to justify his answer. The group should try to agree on one answer or interpretation.
> 3 The groups exchange partners and students compare their results.
> 4 A general discussion involving the whole class may follow.
> (Grellet 1983: 11)

► # TASK 32

Consider each of the organizational patterns outlined above and draw up a list of advantages and disadvantages for each one. You may like to think about some or all of the following:

> general behaviour of the group
> possibilities for communication between learners
> the expectations of the learner with regard to the teacher's physical position in the classroom
> suitability for different types of language learning activities (for a list, see Task 35).

Another strategy is to give the learners the choice of working modes, or the choice of learning materials. We shall examine this when we turn to the *learner's strategies and tasks* later in this section.

Teachers' personalities

Many authorities believe that teaching style is fundamentally a matter of personality. For example, examine the quotes that follow:

> 1 ... in the main, your style of teaching will depend on the sort of person you are.
> (Gower and Walters 1983: 7)

> 2 ... some people are born teachers, who have the desire and the ability to pass knowledge and skills on successfully. But even a person who is not a born teacher can improve a lot by learning to smile, to be enthusiastic and patient, and to be constantly looking for new ways of getting his message across to his pupils.
> (Hill and Dobbyn 1982: 30)

> 3 As regards discipline: this basically depends on the personality of the teacher, her class, and the relationship between them, not on the type of activity. On the whole it is safe to say that a class which is controlled in frontal work will be controlled also in groups.
> (Ur 1981: 8)

Think about the questions which follow.

> 1 Is it true to say that one's personality is the main influence on teaching style?
> 2 Do you agree that a smiling face will contribute to better and more efficient teaching?
> 3 Do you think that the quality of the relationship in the classroom is the major contributory factor in classroom discipline? Can you think of any activities which can improve the teacher/learner relationship?

It is too simple to state, for example, that 'a warm, sunny teacher personality' will create a 'warm and productive classroom climate'?

It may be true that teachers who are predisposed towards communicating with others and who are interested in learners as people are more likely to succeed in the classroom than those who regard teaching only as the routine transmission of knowledge. On the other hand, a teaching style that is centred on personal relationships rather than learning tasks can only succeed if the learning group accepts such a strategy, or the school authorities sanction such behaviour, or parents and other sponsors believe this to be in the best interests of the learner.

It is worth considering whether we can modify our personalities to suit different circumstances. We can only do this if we have a greater awareness of the social psychological reality of the classroom.

Do you for example agree with the views of Edwards?

> Classrooms are, or have been, status-marked situations in which personal feelings and personalized responses are largely ignored. (Edwards 1976: 170)

Although many authorities agree with the sentiments expressed by Edwards, there are some who believe that the situation need not be as he describes it.

► TASK 33

Study the following steps suggested by Stevick (1980) so that teachers are better able to encourage their learners to 'perform', i.e. to participate, in classroom activities.

1 How relevant are these ideas to you personally?

2 Do you believe that by following these steps you would develop as a teacher?

3 What risks would you run if you tried to implement any of these in your present working situation?

4 Could you turn any of them into practical action in the classroom?

5 How would they help the learner to develop and what aspects of the learner would they develop?

> Study the students' motivation, attitudes, and the social pressures on them in order to build up a fuller picture of them as people.
>
> Scrutinize your methods and techniques in terms of the amount of control we provide and the amount of student-led activity there is.
>
> Give more control and responsibility to the learners.

Think positively and communicate this to the learners.

Act 'normally' in class, as another participant in the process, rather than as a 'teacher'.

Become less evaluative of the learners' efforts, allowing them more time to be evaluative of their own.

Give students the chance to discuss and evaluate the course, the language, their fears, and frustrations.

Teachers' attitudes and beliefs

The teacher's style is inevitably going to be influenced by his beliefs and attitudes. These include:

1 cultural and social beliefs and attitudes about how to behave in social groups
2 beliefs about the role of knowledge in teaching and learning
3 beliefs about the nature of learning
4 beliefs about the nature of knowledge (in the case of language teachers, a view of language).

Research by Barnes (1969, 1976) has identified two basic types of teacher. These are not absolute opposites, but are tendencies towards one extreme or the other.

As you read through these, indicate whether or not you agree with each statement, i.e. whether or not you believe them.

Transmission teachers believe that:

there are distinctive disciplines such as science and foreign languages;

there are very distinct boundaries between these disciplines;

the disciplines have 'content' or 'things to learn';

there are appropriate standards of performance in each discipline;

learners' performance can be evaluated according to the standards laid down by the discipline;

the teacher's main task is to evaluate and correct learners' performance;

learners should find it difficult to gain access to the discipline because of the standards the teachers lay down.

Interpretation teachers believe that:

knowledge is the ability to organize thought, to interpret facts, and to act on them;

learners are intrinsically interested and naturally inclined to explore their worlds;

the teacher's main task is to set up dialogues in which learners reorganize their existing state of knowledge;

learners already know a great deal and also have the ability to extend
and refashion that knowledge.
(Adapted from Barnes 1976)

These two different sets of beliefs have several implications for teaching
style and classroom management activities.

A transmission teacher will need to maintain a high degree of control over
his learners in order to create the conditions under which the discipline can
be taught. A teacher of this type will reward contributions from the learners
that he approves of within the bounds set by the discipline of, say, maths or
history. Learners must conform or fail. The 'subject' is central and the
teacher embodies the subject, almost as a protector of the body of
knowledge that he is teaching. Results in examinations are the criterion of
the teacher's success.

An interpretation teacher would prefer to disperse responsibility for
learning among the learners. Control is maintained by persuasion and
appeal to the better judgement of the learners. The teacher's position is, in
terms of the amount of control he exerts over the learners, weaker than that
of the transmission teacher. Learners develop their knowledge of the
subject and also refine their personalities. Understanding is the criterion of
the teacher's success.

There are other hidden roles within both characterizations of the teacher
drawn up by Barnes.

1 The teacher is an *evaluator* of learners' efforts and contributions. The
   teacher judges whether learners' contributions to the teaching/learning
   process are valid, relevant, correct.

2 The teacher is a *guide* to the 'subject' under consideration and the way in
   which it is learnt in the classroom. He is also the curator of the 'rules' for
   acquiring knowledge.

3 Closely linked to the 'guide' role is the role of *resource*. The teacher is a
   resource of knowledge about the subject and also how to acquire it.

4 The teacher is also, as implied by (2) and (3), an *organizer*. The teacher
   organizes classroom activities, sets up learning tasks and assists the
   learners in doing these activities.

▶ **TASK 34**

Look again at the descriptions of the transmission and the
interpretation teacher and decide which features imply the four
hidden roles outlined above.

What conclusions do you draw for the management role of each type
of teacher?

Which style do you regard as most risky?

Which style is most prevalent in your culture? Are there any reasons for its prevalence?

Look at the discussion of *personal motivation* in Section One. Can you see any parallels between the beliefs and attitudes of McGregor's Theory X and Theory Y organizations and the types of teacher described above?

The beliefs and attitudes of the teacher are obviously going to be realized in classroom action. The way a lesson is planned and run will give clues about a teacher's attitudes towards the learning task and the role of knowledge.

▶ # TASK 35

Look at the lesson outlines which follow. Which teacher do you think has a tendency towards transmission and which teacher has a tendency towards interpretation? What evidence can you find?

TASKS FOURTEEN TO SEVENTEEN—
SEQUENCING AND RETELLING OF ANECDOTES

(a) Pre-teach necessary vocabulary.

(b) Give each student his or her slip of paper.

(c) Ask each person to learn his part of the text by heart.

(d) Check with individuals that they fully understand their parts of the text, and that they have memorised them.

(e) Collect all the slips of paper in.

(f) Ask the students to stand up and move around the classroom. If you have heavy, fixed furniture, get the students to use the front, back and sides of the room. Tell them to try and get into little groups that correspond to their story by saying their part of the story to each other.

(g) When everbody has found the right group, tell them that <u>every member</u> of a group must be able to tell the group's anecdote clearly and adequately. Give them time to achieve this.

(h) Pair students from the different story groups so that they can tell their story to someone who does not yet know it.

(Rinvolucri 1980: 84)

STAGE	TEACHER	LEARNERS	COMMENT
1	Tells the class they are going to read about James Cook. Asks them what they know about him.	Respond with a few details about Cook.	Anticipation work. A few details are sufficient for this preliminary work.
2	Tells the class to find the following key phrases which will help them to get the gist of the first four paragraphs: —the greatest English explorer —worked on a farm —ran away to sea —learned the art of navigation —the Royal Navy —he took command of the *Endeavour* —a scientific expedition —the supposed purpose —its real purpose	Find the key phrases.	Highlighting key phrases as a help to identifying the main ideas.
3	Asks the class now to read quickly the first four paragraphs in order to give a title to each paragraph.	Read lines 1–27 and write down four titles.	Practice in identifying the main ideas. Type of reading: skimming.
4	Discusses with learners the suitability of titles, e.g. Paragraph 1: A great explorer Paragraph 2: His youth	Give titles.	To confirm or revise learners' understanding of the gist of these four paragraphs.

STAGE	TEACHER	LEARNERS	COMMENT
	Paragraph 3: Life in the Royal Navy Paragraph 4: The *Endeavour* expedition		
5	Provides on **BB** or on a handout a simplified map of the South Pacific area (Australia, New Zealand, Tahiti, Java).	Copy map from **BB**, if no handout provided.	A preliminary to some transfer of information work.
6	Asks class to read the last paragraph and draw the route Cook took. Circulates round the room to check on performance.	Draw the route by extracting information from last paragraph.	Type of reading has changed from skimming (lines 1–27) to study reading. This is to provide: 1: a change of activity and 2: practice in another reading skill. Note that a specific purpose has been provided before learners read the paragraph.
7	Now asks one learner to draw his route on **BB** and checks its accuracy with class. Refers class to the text if there is any doubt, discrepancy, etc.	One learner draws his route on **BB**. Other learners comment on its accuracy, and, if necessary, provide the correct version.	Confirmation or revision of learners' comprehension. Constant reference back to the text itself.
8	Asks class to read the last paragraph a second time and	Read a second time and write in the verbs.	A second reading requires a different purpose, to be effective.

STAGE	TEACHER	LEARNERS	COMMENT
	write in all the Simple Past Tense verbs at the correct points on the route map.		Further study reading.
9	Elicits verbs from learners while he writes them up on BB at the appropriate points. As he writes the verbs, he utters a full sentence, e.g. Yes. He turned west.	Provide verbs for BB. Check the points where verbs are written.	Immediate feedback. Learners hear as well as see the sequence of events on Cook's voyage.
10	Asks individual learners to recount the events of the voyage by looking either at BB or their own version, but with the full text covered.	Different learners recount the voyage orally.	Not memorisation of the text, but an oral account of part of the last paragraph. The transfer of information work provides adequate stimulus/cues. Note here, and in other stages, practice of the listening and speaking skills in a subordinate role.
11	Asks class to write out the account, with reference only to the information on their maps.	Write the account of the voyage.	Initial written follow-up. Further work could be provided by writing a similar report of another voyage.

(Abbot and Wingard 1981: 104–6)

Now consider the list of language learning activities which follows. Which activities would seem to derive from a transmission view of teaching and which derive from an interpretation view?

group composition
structure drills
transformation exercises for grammar points
role play in which roles are set up by the teacher or textbook
simulations
reading comprehension
learning lists of vocabulary for tests
dictation
open-ended discussion

Are there any that you cannot categorize accurately? Do you find yourself saying 'But it depends . . .'? If you do, what do your doubts depend on?

Teaching style: summary

Teaching style is a complex amalgam of belief, attitude, strategy, technique, motivation, personality, and control. It is usually worked out in response to the language teaching/learning situations in which teachers find themselves employed. There is more to classroom management than discipline or seating arrangements: teaching style lies at the heart of the interpersonal relationship between teacher and learner. However, a basic set of factors lies behind teaching style. These relate to:

attitudes towards knowledge and learning;
preferred means of maintaining control over learners;
preferred ways of organizing class activities;
positive or negative feelings about teaching itself;
beliefs about the purpose of education in general;
influences from within the teacher's role set;
tendencies towards behaviour which favours the taking of risks or towards conformist behaviour;
beliefs about the best ways of learning a language;
attitudes towards learners.

Before moving to another part of this section, you might pause and consider this quote from a leading observer of classroom life:

Stray thoughts, sudden insights, meandering digressions, irrelevant asides, and other minor disruptions constantly ruffle the smoothness of the instructional dialogue. Experienced teachers accept this state of affairs and come to look upon surprise and uncertainty as natural features in their environment. They know, or come to know that the path of educational progress more closely resembles the flight of a butterfly than the flight of a bullet.
(Jackson 1968: 167)

As well as the managerial role, the teacher has an instructional role. What are the implications for both roles of the comments in Jackson's statement? How do Jackson's observations match with your perceptions of the process of learning a foreign language in the classroom?

3.2 Instructional tasks and instructional strategies

The instructional side of a teacher's role is likely to be

goal-oriented
task-dependent
knowledge-based

and underpinned by a set of attitudes and beliefs, not only about knowledge, but also the appropriate instructional strategies to employ in the classroom. Furthermore, it is likely to influence the types and modes of evaluation most favoured by teachers.

We shall now scrutinize the instructional role from three broad perspectives:

1 modes of instruction
2 instructional materials and resources
3 the management of knowledge.

Modes of instruction

A teacher can pursue his instructional role in a variety of modes. It is rare for a classroom language teacher to stick to only one mode during the course of a lesson. However, teachers tend to favour particular modes of instruction which suit either

the personality of the teacher
the materials being used
the expectations of the learners
the prescriptions of school administrators
the subject matter being treated
the preferences of teachers for certain types of classroom process
the teacher's interpretation of the idea of 'instruction'

▶ TASK 36

1 How far does your idea of instruction match with the ideas expressed in the extracts below?

a. . . . the teacher *instructs*. This is where he explains exactly what the students should do. He may tell the students they are going to work in pairs and then designate one member of each pair as **A** and the other as **B**.
(Harmer 1983: 203)

b. ... most importantly the teacher is in the classroom as a facilitator of the process of communication between the learners, their tasks, and the data to which the various tasks are directed. (Abbs, Candlin, Edelhoff, Moston, and Sexton 1982: ix)

2 What do *you* believe instruction consists of?
3 Do you think the first author's ideas about instruction are sufficient?
4 How much is instruction a matter of organization and how much is it a matter of finding ways for learners to acquire knowledge?

Now examine the descriptions of some of the possible instructional modes which follow. Do this with the context of the transmission and the interpretation teacher in mind. Ask yourself which types of teacher would prefer each of the various modes of instruction.

Lecture: The teacher expounds at length on a topic. Learners listen and may take notes. The lecture can be interrupted by questions from the learners, but these normally occur at the end of the lecture.

A 'mini lecture' is also used quite frequently, to explain what appears to be a misunderstood concept, for example, 'explaining' is often a form of mini lecture.
For example:

> T ... prevented + you see is followed by + from + not directly + you cannot say prevented + eeh + it also prevented from essential foodstuffs from being exported + thats not correct + it also prevented essential foodstuffs from being exported + any other problem? ... so this + the idea then + is plain + prote-protect against + and you prevent from + the government protected home industries against foreign competition by taxing imports + it also prevented essential foodstuffs from being exported ... protect against prevent from ...
> (Wright, in preparation)

Elicitation: Teachers probe the learners through close questioning in order to bring previously acquired knowledge to the surface. In this way teachers either clarify that knowledge or get learners to say or do something with the knowledge as a prelude to embarking on new knowledge.

> Instead of just 'presenting' the language to the students (e.g. by telling them or writing it on the board), the teacher elicits the relevant information from the students by asking questions. The presentation material may take the form of examples, a listening dialogue or reading passage, or even pictures, and the teacher uses this and his own questions to establish the teaching point or to introduce new items of language.
> (Doff, Jones, Mitchell 1983: 15)

Evaluation: The means by which teachers assess what the learners already know or have learnt as a result of the new language having been presented through question and answer routines. Example:

> T What kind of word is *always*?
> P An adverb.
> T Good. And *wonderful*?
> (Sinclair and Brazil 1982: 53)

Lockstep: The teacher leads the class through a tightly controlled sequence of activities centred on a new language point. All the learners work at the same pace under the direction of the teacher. Example:

> Teacher: They drank champagne – beer.
> Students: They drank beer.
> Teacher: coffee
> Students: They drank coffee.
> Teacher: tea
> Students: They drank tea.
> (Hubbard, Jones, Thornton, and Wheeler 1983: 21)

A drill of this type may be part of a sequence of activities over which the teacher has complete control. Evaluation may well form a considerable part of the follow up to the drill illustrated and lockstep is best used to describe a lesson rather than a single activity.

All these modes share two key features:

> the control of the teacher over the activity
> the whole-class grouping, all learners focused on the teacher or an individual member of the class.

▶ # TASK 37

1 How appropriate are any of the above modes for the teaching of the following:

> grammar, pronunciation, vocabulary, speaking, listening, writing, reading?

2 Would you say that the modes illustrated are best suited for the teaching of skills (reading, writing, speaking, listening) or systems (grammar, pronunciation, vocabulary)?

3 Would it be fair to say that any of these modes is and can be used by teachers as means of controlling learners' behaviour, i.e. 'keeping them quiet or occupied'?

An alternative: inquiry-centred learning

It is likely that the modes outlined above are favoured by the transmission teacher. An alternative is *inquiry-centred* learning. Its main procedures include the following:

1 The teacher plans in advance the topics and ideas that the class may wish to explore. The teacher then organizes a sequence of teaching/learning activities around them.

2 The teacher introduces the new material and challenges the learners to try out and explore new ideas.

3 The teacher insists on the communication of ideas and beliefs from the class and justifications for opinions expressed.

4 The teacher recaps, summarizes, and asks for clarification as and when necessary.

5 The teacher gives the learners the opportunity to guess and 'play hunches'.

6 The class is organized into small working groups.

The basic assumption is that learners will learn more if they are given opportunities to participate in discovering ideas for themselves.

New roles are implied by this approach. The teacher is primarily a facilitator, setting up tasks and providing the instructional materials. He is also a guide to the process of discovery and understanding. The teacher is also still an assessor (see 4 above) but only in so far as he is helping to clarify concepts and knowledge where it seems to be appropriate. In this approach much is made of the learners' own ideas and beliefs which the teacher attempts to refashion if it appears to be necessary.

In inquiry-centred learning the process of learning is seen to be as important as the content of learning. This contrasts with the emphasis on *knowledge* in approaches such as the lecture mode.

Consider this extract:

> Perceiving the learners as having important contributions to make – in terms of initial competence and a range of various and changing expectations – can enable the teacher to continually seek potential and exploit it.
> (Breen and Candlin 1980: 99)

How do you see the teacher's role in the light of such comments?

► TASK 38

What are the implications of inquiry-centred learning for language teaching?

1 What is there in language that could be the basis of inquiry?

2 What sort of tasks is the teacher going to set language learners in an inquiry-centred classroom?

3 What new demands is such an approach going to make on a teacher and on the learners?

4 What sorts of linguistic and communicative features can learners be encouraged to make guesses at?

5 Would such an approach lead to a redistribution of power in the classroom?

6 Would the teacher's status be 'at risk' with such an approach?

7 Could you foresee every language class being organized on this basis?

8 What types of instructional material and resources would be required?

9 Could the outcomes of activities in such an instructional mode be predicted in advance? What advantages and disadvantages do you foresee?

10 Could you conceive of an instructional mode which blended the best features of the inquiry-centred approach and the more content-focused modes?

► TASK 39

1 How far does the material which follows go towards achieving the ends of inquiry-centred learning?

2 How might it be employed with reference to the outline of the procedures of inquiry-centred learning you have looked at?

OH TO BE IN ENGLAND

1 Work in groups. What do you think the climate is like in the places marked on the map? How do they compare with your own town or city? Can you guess which is the hottest and which is the coldest place? And which is the wettest and which is the driest?

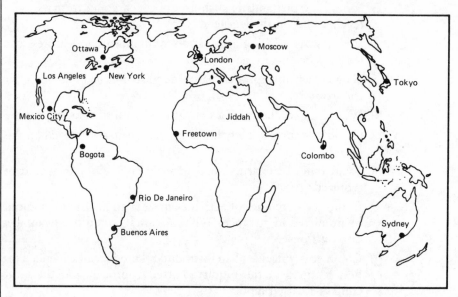

2 When you have made your guesses, half the members of the group should look at communication activity 14, while the others look at activity 27. You will find more details and information there. The communication activities are at the back of the book.

What's the weather like in . . .?	*It doesn't sound very nice in . . .*
Do you think it's very . . . in . . .?	*It sounds much too . . . for me.*
I should think the coldest month is . . .	*It's probably quite pleasant in . . .*

(Jones 1984: 12)

3.3 Instructional materials and resources

Here we shall look at the factors which influence the choice of teaching materials and the ways in which these are designed.

These will be grouped under two broad headings:

1 factors related to general beliefs and attitudes about education, i.e. what is language teaching for?

and

2 attitudes and beliefs about the role of knowledge itself, and the type of knowledge that forms the basis of classroom language learning activities, i.e. what is language and how is it best learnt?

Look at the three views below. They all show different approaches to the question of the role and content of teaching materials.

1 Learning activities will not be of much help to the learner of English unless they present and practise English in a systematic and comprehensive way so that new language items can be assimilated by the learner.
(Cunningsworth 1984: 6–7)

2 It has been customary, [. . .], to base language teaching materials on a previously decided list of items, whether language-based or skills-based. These 'a priori' syllabuses assume a need on the part of the teacher, textbook writer, and others, to select and order the material to be presented, usually in terms of its linguistic usefulness or frequency. [. . .]

An alternative procedure would be to devise a series of intersecting activities using more or less authentic texts.
(Grellet, Maley, and Welsing 1982: 7)

3 Materials should have twin aims: on the one hand they offer information and data about the language being studied, and in particular about the social context and the culture within which communication takes place and derives much of its meaning and value. They need, in this sense, to be authentic to communication and to the world outside the classroom. At the same time, materials have a role to promote learning and language learning in particular. They fulfil this role in the way they offer activities and tasks and exercises which challenge the competence of the learners . . .
(Candlin and Edelhoff 1982: x)

We want to answer two questions:

1 What influences our choice of teaching materials?
2 What part do we want teaching materials to play in the classroom learning process?

Beliefs and attitudes about the nature of education

The 'school of thought' or discipline in which a teacher is trained or the group among whom he cuts his teeth as a practitioner will undoubtedly influence his ideas about teacher and learner roles. This set of beliefs and attitudes is likely to be reinforced by views about the role of teaching materials, including textbooks, in the language classroom.

Are teaching materials the servant or the master of the language teaching/learning process?

In order to answer this question we need to have a view on what the goals of language teaching are and to what extent the materials we use lead to the achievement of these goals. One commonly held view is that the teaching of the materials is the primary goal; hence the attitude that materials should cover the syllabus.

There are two major problems with such a view:

1 It is difficult for teachers to prevent 'other material' entering the classroom process, such as the learners' feelings and desires to contribute from their own experience and knowledge of the world.

2 There is a very heavy responsibility on the teacher for providing the means and stating the ends of learning.

An alternative view is that teaching materials are only a means to an end. Teachers use certain materials because they help to promote language learning. Such a view would lead to the conclusion that teachers are best left to the fostering of a good classroom climate while the learners work on the materials.

There are problems with this view, too.

1 If teachers have no influence over the writing of the materials, the materials may not suit either their own or the learners' purposes.

2 Teachers may complain that if the stages of the instructional process are encapsulated in the materials, then they are reduced to the role of interpreters of a script.

▶ **TASK 40**

What do *you* think about teaching materials?
Examine the series of statements which follows. How far do you agree or disagree with them? Note down your answers and keep them for reference.

1 Teaching materials should contain plenty of exercises to practise language skills such as speaking, writing, listening, and reading.

2 Teaching materials should be under the control of teachers at all times.

3 Teaching materials should not be permanent: they should be disposable or alterable to suit learner needs and choices.

4 Teaching materials should contain samples of authentic language data.

5 Teaching materials should be flexible to allow learners the chance to work at their own speed and in their own preferred ways.

6 Teaching materials should allow variable outcomes, in terms of solutions to problems or tasks.

7 Teaching materials are indispensable.

8 Teaching materials are really unnecessary; learners can learn from each other and the teacher without recourse to printed material.

9 Teaching materials should offer plenty of guidance to both teachers and learners in terms of the tasks they should perform and how they should perform them.

10 Teaching materials should set up contexts in which learners can express themselves, their own opinions, ideas, and attitudes.

What types of information are there in teaching materials? Teaching materials contain, either overtly or covertly, the following important information:

information about the content of language learning, be it structural, discoursal, or skills-oriented (language data)

information about the likely methods the teacher should employ in the classroom

information about the target culture

information about learning processes to be fostered among the learners (classroom organization).

Study the sample material which follows. Each type of information is marked for your attention.

(Doff, Jones, and Mitchell 1983: 9)

Think about this:

> Which do *you* think is the most important sort of information that teaching materials should contain?

As we saw in the discussion of transmission and interpretation teachers, both hold strong views regarding the role of knowledge and how it is to be acquired and evaluated. We have noted that teaching materials contain both implicit and explicit statements about the type of knowledge to be acquired. All this has relevance to the teacher's instructional role because of the knowledge he is assumed to have at his disposal.

What are the broad types of language teaching material?

A Language study = study of structures

This type of material is likely to place a heavy emphasis on grammatical rules and formulae. The emphasis will be on the acquisition of correct grammatical forms, with exercises geared towards the provision of 'the right answer', e.g. blank-filling, drills, substitution tables. The implied arbiter of correctness is the teacher who will often have an answer book for the exercises.

---

50 **will** + infinitive and the **be going to** form

Future with intention can usually be expressed by **will** + infinitive or the **be going to** form. Very often either of these can be used, but when the intention is clearly premeditated the **be going to** form must be used, and when the intention is clearly unpremeditated we must use **will** + infinitive.

Put the verbs in brackets into one of these two forms. (In some of the examples the present continuous could be used instead of the **be going to** form.)

1 The fire has gone out! ~
  So it has. I (go) and get some sticks.
2 Did you remember to book seats? ~
  Oh no, I forgot. I (telephone) for them now.
3 He has just been taken to hospital with a broken leg. ~
  I'm sorry to hear that. I (send) him some grapes.
4 I've hired a typewriter and I (learn) to type.
5 I see that you have got a loom. You (do) some weaving?
6 I can't understand this letter. ~
  I (call) my son. He (translate) it for you.
7 You (buy) meat? ~
  No, I (not eat) meat any more. I (eat) vegetables.
8 You've bought a lot of paint. You (redecorate) your kitchen?

(Thomson and Martinet 1986: 79–80)

B Language study = study of language in situations

Target situations and the language that learners need in these situations are
the focus of this type of material. The situation may be 'social' or more
specifically work- or study-oriented. A variety of exercise types and
activities are possible, but it is generally the teacher who decides on the
criteria for appropriacy, even if he is only conveying the message contained
in the materials: these will usually give him the licence to do so. Example:

> Defining ESL
> English as a second language provision is designed for people living,
> working, and bringing up families in this country. Like all adults
> they need to:
> a. make informed choices about their own lives and the lives of
>   their children
> b. be able to take advantage of any opportunities for further
>   education and training
> c. understand the institutions and structures of the society in which
>   they live so that they may play an active part in it if they so wish.
> [. . .]
> In order to cope in the many situations they may meet, these second
> language speakers need a complex range of interrelated communica-
> tion, literacy, and access skills.
> (Nicholls and Naish 1981: 12–13)

C Language study = study of language as a system of communicative
   functions

This type of material claims to focus on the use of language as a means of
transmitting attitudes and concepts and for 'getting things done'. The
language is presented in but not tied to situations—transfer to parallel
situations is an implied learning task. Typical means of presenting the
language are employed (drills, dialogues, etc.) along with such techniques
as controlled and free role play, controlled group discussions, and the like.
Less depends on the teacher in the 'free' stages of the material, but the
sequencing of learning tasks from controlled to free is reliant upon the
teacher's management and instructional skills. Example:

> The functional approach provides a means of organizing all the
> material that must be mastered before a person can be said to have
> 'learnt a language'. The approach involves isolating certain
> *language functions*, such as 'asking for information' . . .
> (Jones 1981: 1)

B Inviting

B1 Read and study.

> Would you like to go to the cinema with me tonight?

> Sorry, I'm afraid I can't.
> I'm playing tennis.
> I don't like the cinema.

or

> Yes, I'd love to!
> that would be nice.
> all right.

B2 In pairs, take turns to invite each other to do these things. Answer truthfully!

go to the cinema
go to the beach
go to a club
go to a disco
go out for a meal
go out for a drink
go out for a walk
come to lunch
come to dinner
come to my house

B3 This is your diary for the week. Find someone in the class to do these things with you:

go for a walk	go to a disco
go to a concert	spend a quiet evening at
go to the cinema	home
have dinner	play tennis

Fill your diary. But you must not do the same thing twice in the week. And you must not see the same person twice in the week.

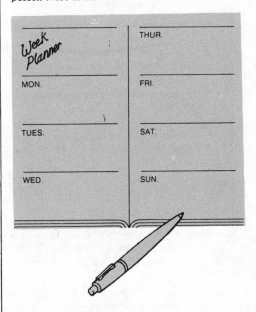

Week Planner

MON.   THUR.

TUES.   FRI.

WED.   SAT.

        SUN.

C What are you going to do?

C1 🔊 In the school café. Listen and study.
What is Rosa going to do?

> What are you going to do after the course?

> I'm going to .... a bit. What are you going to do?

> I'm going to look for another job.

C2 What are your plans for the future?
What are you going to do . . .

– this weekend?
– during the course?
– next week?
– after the course?
– when you go home?

(Black, McNorton, Malderez, and Parker 1986: 47)

2.2 Presentation: question techniques

A conversation often depends on questions to keep it going in the direction you want it to go. The one who asks the questions in a conversation usually controls the conversation. Various techniques may be necessary to get different sorts of information from different people. Most people are very polite in the way they ask a stranger about something – if you are more direct, you may appear to be very rude! Anyway, personal questions have to be expressed tactfully. Here are some useful opening expressions you can use to lead up to questions:

I was wondering if you could help me. I'd like to know . . .
I wonder if you could tell me . . .
This may sound a stupid question, but I'd like to know . . .
Excuse me, do you happen to know . . .
Would you mind telling me . . .
I hope you don't mind my asking, but I'd like to know . . .
Something else I'd like to know is . . .

Decide when such expressions might be appropriate. They are also useful as 'hesitation devices' to give you time to prepare your thoughts!

2.3 Practice

Note down about five pieces of factual information and five pieces of personal information you would like from your teacher. Take turns asking your teacher questions: remember to be very polite when asking for personal information. When you have finished, ask a partner similar questions.

(Jones 1981: 10)

D Language study = study of the communicative potential of language

Although there may be elements of this type of material in type C materials, these materials are less reliant on the teacher for their success. The materials may originally have set up the exercises and tasks, but these necessitate the learners actually deciding the order in which they can be done or even how they are to be done. The teacher is a guide, a resource (he can be consulted by the learners) and an assistant. Successful completion of tasks depends less on the teacher's and more on the learners' efforts. Knowledge about the language is 'discovered' in the course of study. Example:

STEP 1 READING

It is not easy to find a job. One way is to look at the advertisements in a newspaper. Here are some advertisements from an English newspaper.

SITUATIONS VACANT

At Britain's friendliest Bank we've room for a few more friendly faces.

If you're between the ages of 16 and 19 with a good general education, there is a place waiting for you as a Bank Clerk with the **NORTHLAND BANK.**

It is an interesting job with security, variety and responsibility, not to mention job satisfaction. The conditions of work are good and the job advancement prospects are excellent.

Feel you'd like to be a part of Britain's Friendliest Bank? Apply in writing to:
**THE MANAGER
NORTHLAND
BANK**
14 CAMBRIA ROAD
ROCKTON
RO1 9PI

WISELY OF MORECAMBE

require

Sales Assistant

for Gifts. Handbags, etc., 10 am to 7 pm, 5 days.
Please apply in person.

30 HIGH STREET, MORECAMBE

Next to Winter Gardens.

UNIVERSITY BOOKSHOP

Mature Person

required to join staff of privately run bookshop on University Campus. Experience of book trade preferable but not essential. Apply in writing to:-

**The Manager
Students
Bookshops Ltd.,**
UNIVERSITY BOOKSHOP
COLMINSTER

LADY REQUIRED

to look after
ELDERLY GENTLEMAN
Nursing experience
desirable
Mon. to Fri.
8.30 am to 4.30 pm or
HALF DAYS

BOX No 681

STRONG YOUTH WANTED
for
General Farm work
Some experience essential
LANCASTER AREA
Apply—
Box No 30

WEST END, MORECAMBE
**Waitress/
General Help**
REQUIRED
Approx 20 hours per week

ABBEY HOTEL
COLMINSTER
REQUIRE
**PART-TIME
BAR STAFF**
(for evenings)
also
PART-TIME COOK
OR
CHAMBERMAID
(Male or Female)
6 mornings per week
8 to 11 am
Experience preferred
Apply in person
ABBEY HOTEL
CROSS STREET
COLMINSTER

WANTED

Clerk Typist

for
LANCASTER FIRM
Aged 35 to 45 years
Used to accounts etc

BOX No 31

PART-TIME
GARDENER/
HANDYMAN
REQUIRED
Please tel Hornby 6397

JOBS AT SEA
Go where the money is on
a North Sea Oil Drilling Rig
or
travel the world on an
OCEAN LINER
Men and women wanted
Experience unnecessary
SEND 65p now for
EMPLOYMENT GUIDE to:
OPPORTUNITY INTERNATIONAL
LIMITED
II MARINE ROAD

(Abbs, Candlin, Edelhoff, Moston, and Sexton 1981: 42)

Ask each other these questions about the jobs in the newspaper.

Make up more questions yourselves.

Which jobs are suitable for someone who likes working outdoors?
Which jobs are good for people who enjoy meeting other people?
Which jobs involve spending a lot of hours sitting down?
Which jobs involve irregular hours?
Which jobs need a lot of patience?
Which job is suitable for someone who likes reading?
Which job is suitable for someone who likes travelling?

Read the Situations Vacant section of the newspaper. Note down a job which interests you and how to apply.

TASK 1

Some of the advertisements ask you to apply in writing. Here is a model of a letter of application. Choose the job you wish to apply for, and complete the letter of application. Invent any necessary details.

ADDRESS OF THE PEOPLE YOU ARE WRITING TO

YOUR ADDRESS

THE DATE

Dear Sir,

With reference to your advertisement in The_____(name of newspaper) of_____(date), I would like to apply for the vacancy as a_____(job).

I am_____(age). I left school after the_____(class). Since leaving school I have had_____(number of jobs).

I will be free from_____(date) and hope to start work on_____(date). I am interested in working as a_____(job) because_____ _____(reasons). I will be available for interview_____ _____(dates and times).

I look forward to hearing from you.

Yours faithfully,

SIGNATURE

YOUR NAME PRINTED

TASK 2

Employers often send application forms to people who reply to their advertisements. Imagine that you receive this form in reply to the letter you wrote for Task 1. Fill in the form.

APPLICATION FORM

APPLICANT'S NAME   (Block capitals please, with surname first).

HOME ADDRESS

AGE LAST BIRTHDAY
VACANCY APPLIED FOR

EDUCATION
PREVIOUS EXPERIENCE
REASON FOR LEAVING
LAST JOB

State your reasons for applying for the vacancy. Use a separate page if necessary.

(Abbs, Candlin, Edelhoff, Moston, and Sexton 1981: 43)

E Language study = exploration of personal feelings and attitudes and their expression in the target language

Language is seen as a means to an end, not as an end in itself. Tasks are set up with the express purpose of inviting personal statements from the learners and maybe the teacher, too. There are no rules as to the form of the language that is to be produced—it is the message that counts. Self-discovery and the appreciation of the feelings of others are emphasized. Values and emotions are paramount. Example:

> *Speaking Personally* aims to help learners to improve their competence in social communication skills. [. . .] Underlying the material is the conviction that people will learn more readily and efficiently if they are actively and personally involved in their language lessons.
> (Porter Ladousse 1983: 1)

3.2   Honest geography

Honesty is very often a relative concept and depends on conventions in different societies. For instance, bribery is considered very bad in some countries whereas in others it is almost institutionalised. Stealing is considered a greater or lesser crime depending on where you live, and some people say that the dishonesty of a politician like Richard Nixon would not have brought about his downfall in any other country but the United States of America. On the world map below pin-point any parts of the globe that you know of that have particularly honest or dishonest principles. Work with a partner.

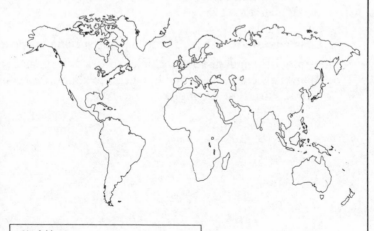

Useful language

incorruptible	bribery, corruption
trustworthy	untrustworthy
scrupulous	unscrupulous
	a lie, a fib
	a confidence trick
to be reliable	to trick
to have principles	to double cross
to be upright	to fiddle
	to swindle

to have something on one's conscience
to give someone the benefit of the doubt

(Porter Ladousse 1983: 14)

F Language study = study and acquisition of skills in the target language

The focus is on the skills of speaking, listening, reading, and writing. Activities are designed to assist learners in developing one or more of these skills. The emphasis is on the skill rather than the linguistic forms. Example:

> *Streamline English* adopts as its first principle the maxim that people learn to do something by doing it.
> People learn to listen by listening.
> People learn to speak by speaking.
> People learn to read by reading.
> People learn to write by writing.
> (Hartley and Viney 1982: 7)

G Language study = problem posing

This is a relatively recent innovation in language teaching which aims to encourage learners to think critically about the world they live in and at the same time to acquire language to solve their day-to-day problems. Example:

> Problem-posing is the tool for developing critical thinking. It is an inductive process that encourages dialogue in the classroom. Teachers formulate questions to encourage students to make their own conclusions about society's values and pressures and to suggest ways for change.
> (Wallerstein 1983: 17)

H Language study = use of language for specific purposes

The study of language for specific purposes takes many forms, from the occupational, e.g. English for hoteliers, to the more general English for Academic Purposes. Example:

Data Analysis and Comment

Study and discuss the following graphs. Then use them as the basis for writing a three-paragraph text entitled *How long will fossil fuels last?*

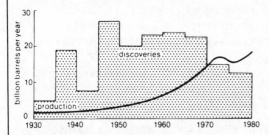

Fig. 6.2 Oil discoveries and production

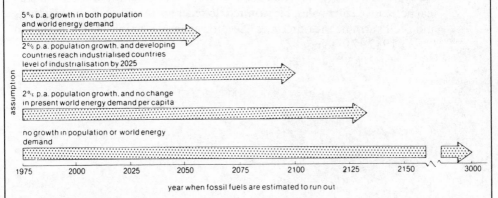

year when fossil fuels are estimated to run out

Fig. 6.3 The estimated life of fossil fuels

The following is a possible text structure:

PARAGRAPH 1: the relationship between discoveries and production:
  – the general trend of discoveries until the 1970s
  – the general trend of production until the 1970s
  – the trend in the 1970s, and its effects
  – projections for the 1980s and 1990s

PARAGRAPH 2: assuming a recovery efficiency of 100%, forecasts of the life of fossil fuels with:
  a) 5% p.a. growth in population and world energy demand.
  b) 2% p.a. population growth, and developing countries reaching the industrialised countries' industrialisation level by 2025
  c) 2% p.a. population growth, and no change in the present world energy demand per capita.
  d) no growth in population or world energy demand.

PARAGRAPH 3: the importance of developing alternative energy sources

Add other comments that you consider relevant. Check your paragraph structure – especially topic sentences, and inter-sentence and inter-paragraph cohesion.

(Williams 1982: 72)

We must also note the link between the linguistic and other goals of the broad objectives outlined above and the broader goals of education:

education as the acquisition of 'objective' knowledge, e.g. grammar (See **A** above.)

education as a means of changing attitudes (See **G** above.)

education as the acquisition of social skills (See **E** above.)

education as the acquisition of skills useful in target situations (See **H** above.)

education as the improvement of communicative skills (See **F** above.)

education as a means of social change (See **G** above.)

How much guidance do materials give to either teacher or learner?
Guidance is usually provided in either the teacher's book or in the rubrics in the student's book. We shall look at both and see how these influence teacher and learner roles. How much do teachers interpret the instructions and predetermine the outcomes? See, for example, Frank, Rinvolucri, and Berer (1982: 7) facing.

THREE-ITEM STORIES

Practice in asking correct questions. Ask questions and find out what the story is which links the three items.

1 Accident/wreckage/no dead or injured

2 Fire/glass/ship

3

4 Pianist/concert/panic

5 Punishment/fence/friends

6

(Frank, Rinvolucri, and Berer 1982: 7)

It is possible to foresee this exercise revolving entirely around the teacher, who acts as a sort of ringmaster, judge of appropriacy of answer and correctness of linguistic forms. Alternatively, the outcome could be extremely open-ended, with all sorts of contributions allowed and any combinations of learners being possible for the achievement of solutions. The point is that the instructions are very vague, whether intentionally or not.

▶ TASK 41

Compare the rubric for the exercise above with the following from a set of teacher's notes.

Which would you prefer to work with and why?

Would the teacher have to invest heavily in motivating the learners to do the exercises in both examples? Would the teacher have to prescribe certain linguistic forms and pre-teach these before the learners started the exercise?

How to use the book – classroom management

The authors' main recommendation is that classroom time is divided equally in three ways: having the students work as a class (listening either to the teacher or to a fellow student), in groups, and individually. Having the students work as a class is most appropriate for introducing a new stage of the unit, discussing answers and drawing conclusions. Group work is preferable wherever students can profit by discussing their ideas with their fellows and will probably be found appropriate for many of the activities in the book. Individual work is most suited to the more controlled type of exercise (particularly writing) where there is less to discuss and it is important that all students should produce a response.

The three types of work can be alternated so as to ensure variety, as is illustrated by the following suggestions:

    I = individual
    G = group
    C = class
    S = students
    T = teacher

UNIT 4 DEFINITIONS
I   Preview S read silently.

PART 1
I-C   T introduces. S study passage and prepare answers to questions 1–7. T asks for oral answers and checks.
C   T goes up to activity 1 reading aloud and asking individual students.

I-C   **Activity 1** is done individually and checked in class.

PART 2
G-C   **Activity 2** The passage is read and discussed and answers are worked out in groups. Answers are checked and explanation is covered in class.

I   **Activity 3**
C-I-C **Activity 4** Explanation is covered in class, and exercise is written individually and checked in class.

PART 3
I-C   **Activity 5**
C-I-C **Activity 6** T does one further example with students and makes sure that procedure for the exercise is understood. Answers are then written individually and checked in class.

PART 4
G-C   **Activity 7**
I-C   **Activity 8** (there is probably less to be discussed here than in activities 7 and 9).
G-C   **Activity 9**

PART 5
C   Go up to the end of the three questions for prediction.
I-C   Reading for purpose is done individually and checked in class.
I-G-C Comprehension questions are discussed and answered in groups after individuals have read the relevant paragraph. Answers are then discussed in class.
I-C   Language study questions.
I-C   Summary writing.

Because much of the book is suitable for individual work, students can be set regular assignments out of class. These can take one of two forms:

a. preparing material (such as a reading passage) for subsequent discussion in class.

b. writing up exercises introduced in class. For instance: an example of an exercise is written up on the board, two more answers are given orally. The teacher is then satisfied that the class knows how to tackle it and sets the whole exercise as a writing assignment.

It is suggested that the teacher should require all written work (including the completion of diagrams, answers to questions, summaries, etc.) to be done in a separate notebook.

DISTRIBUTION OF TIME

The teacher will have to deal with this extremely flexibly, so the following should only be considered as suitable for some circumstances but not for all. The course has been designed to last approximately 60 class periods of 50 minutes plus about 20 out-of-class assignments. This means that the units can be expected to last an average of 10 class periods. Units 3 and 6 may require slightly more than this but the teacher should try and avoid allowing particular units to dominate the others.

(Moore 1979: xviii–xix)

▶   TASK 42

Look at the rubrics of the exercises that follow. Your task is to decide on how open-ended these exercises are and how much the teacher is responsible for the final outcome. Also, what groupings of learners are stated or implied? Can you suggest alternative ways of organizing the learners to do these activities?

CONTEXT AND MEANING

The meaning of a very simple statement depends on who says it, who they are speaking to and where the two people are. Because the people are both in the situation, the meaning is clear to them – it doesn't need to be said. For example:

STATEMENT	MEANING	CONTEXT
'The door is open.'	You forgot to lock it again, idiot!	A bank manager to a clerk standing in front of the safe first thing in the morning.
	What a relief! Now I don't have to sit out here waiting for someone to come home.	A person arrives home without a key, no one is there, the person tries the door and it opens.
	No wonder I'm cold.	A person sitting in a draughty room that is freezing cold.
	Shut the door.	Two people in an office. It's very noisy next door but the speaker doesn't want to get up.
	Please come in.	A receptionist in an office; someone has just rung the bell or knocked.

In each of the following exercises, you are given:

a *a statement and the context it was said in – you say what it means.*
b *a statement and what it means – you supply the context.*
c *a statement – you think of all the meanings and contexts.*

Exercise 1

STATEMENT	MEANING	CONTEXT
a 'It's raining.'		Mother to young son dressed only in T-shirt and shorts who is going outside.
		Farmer to harvesters.
		Noah to his wife.
		Man dying of thirst at sea in a small boat.
		Driver with broken wipers to passenger in car on dark road.

(Frank, Rinvolucri, and Berer 1982: 22)

UNIT 19   *Ability*

*He **could** swim ten miles when he was young.*
*I **was able to** park the car easily this morning.*

1   The following is a real-life horror story. Where exactly do you think
John Brown was when he woke up? Give reasons.

> When he woke up, John Brown could feel his hands tied tightly
> behind his back. Darkness. Why was he lying in this thing and
> breathing through a plastic pipe? And why was there a bottle of
> water on his chest? Then, slowly, he realised the full horror of what
> they had done to him. The car ride. The graveyard. He screamed,
> Nothing. Only the agony of cramp, and dirt in his mouth. But he
> was a yoga expert. After his training he had shown everyone that
> he could control both mind and body almost perfectly. Further, he
> could go without food for long periods. He thanked God for yoga.
> He had precious little else to help him now.

Check   What could John Brown feel when he woke up?
What ability did he have as a result of his yoga training?

2   This is the sequel to John Brown's amazing story.

> He felt a protruding nail at his side. He couldn't turn over, but after
> a while he was able to push his wrists on to the nail. Then started the
> long, painful process of cutting the rope. It was only after two agon-
> ising days of pressing and rubbing that he was able to sever it. He
> cried with relief. He turned over and, although he couldn't push his
> back up far, he had some space. He was able to pull the plastic pipe
> down without loss of air. Then he started hammering. The bottom
> eventually gave way and he was able to dig his way out.

Check   What couldn't John do at first?
What was he able to do after a while?
What was he able to do by pressing and rubbing on the nail?
How did he manage to breathe?
What happened after the bottom gave way?

(Lewis 1984: 94)

Set 1 Household provisions and utensils

1. Have we got any milk? Yes, we've got lots of milk.
Have we got any meat? No, we haven't.

Work in pairs. Look at the kitchen list. Ask and answer like this:
Have we got any ...?
Yes, we've got lots of ....
No, we haven't.

2. Have we got anything to
eat?   We've got some bread.
What else have we got?   We've got some cheese.
What else?

Look at the list again. Ask and answer in the same way.

3. What else have we got? What about tinned
tomatoes?
No, we haven't got any tinned tomatoes.
What about meat?
No, we haven't got any meat.

Look at the things on the list marked with an X. Ask and answer in the same way.

4. Look at the list and say what you have or haven't got at home. Choose only a few things from the list, like this:
I've got some milk, butter and cheese, but I haven't got any fish or meat.

5. Where are the knives
and forks?   In the drawer beside the
cooker.
Which drawer?   The top one.
Where are the cups? In the cupboard on the
top shelf on the left.

Work in pairs. Ask and say exactly where everything is.

cups and saucers	knives, forks and spoons
plates	kitchen knives
bowls	wooden spoons
saucepans	

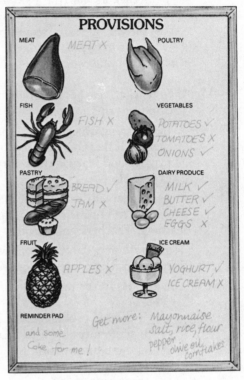

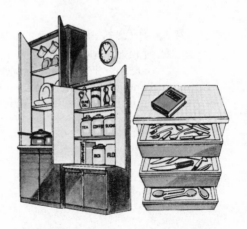

(Abbs and Freebairn 1984: 49)

Do teachers teach with or through materials?
Consider the following extract:

> Teachers can [. . .] be assured that coursebooks from reputable
> publishers will serve them well, if properly selected and used. I used
> the word serve advisedly because coursebooks are good servants but
> poor masters.
> (Cunningsworth 1984: 1)

If a teacher teaches *through* materials, problems may occur. With a
textbook as the 'master':

1 the learning objectives are the textbook's
2 there is little room for improvisation
3 teacher and learner roles may well be predetermined and contrary to
   expectations.

If the teacher teaches *with* the materials, with the textbook as servant, then
he is freer to improvise and adapt the course of lessons to the needs of the
learners. Teachers and learners can also:

1 generate new content from within and from outside the materials;
2 concentrate on interpersonal relationships in the class.

The key lies in the prediction of an outcome of the use of the materials.

> Is there a problem to be posed?
> Is there a problem to be solved?
> Is there information to be found out or discovered?
> How much is the teacher going to direct or lead the learners towards
> these outcomes?

▶ **TASK 43**

Look at the samples of material which follow. Do you think these
are materials to be taught *with* or *through*? What evidence can you
find in the materials themselves and how much do you find yourself
inferring your answers from the layout or rubrics of the exercises?

Unit 5 a

Some, any, a few, a little

1
(a) demonstrators?
(b) policemen?
(c) soldiers?
(d) tourists?
(e) reporters?
(f) birds interested?

2
(a) What/Susan?
(b) What/want to use?
(c) How much sugar usually/always?
(d) chocolate?

3
(a) When/strike?
(b) Where/policemen and strikers?
(c) What day?
(d) What/most of the men?
(e) reporters there?

4
(a) What/Arthur/order?
(b) waiter bring?
(c) many people?

5
(a) How many men?
(b) any women?
(c) What time?
(d) What/Fred?
(e) What/want?
(f) Fred/any money?

(O'Neill, Kingsbury, Yeadon, and Scott 1971a: 26)

SOME, ANY, A FEW, A LITTLE

Unit 5

a

1

This is a small demonstration in a London park. There are some demonstrators and some policemen in the park, but only a few. There are not any soldiers there but there are a few tourists. There are also some reporters there; in fact, there are quite a few. There are also some birds in the trees but they are not very interested in the demonstration.

1. Ask questions with "Are there any . . .?"
   Answer with 'some' or 'not any'
   a) policemen   b) demonstrators
   c) soldiers   d) tourists
   e) reporters   f) birds
2. Now ask questions with "How many . . . are there?"
   Answer with 'a few' or 'quite a few'

2

Susan is going to bake a cake. She has some eggs, butter, sugar and milk. She wants to use only a few eggs and a little butter. She always uses a lot of sugar. She has not got any chocolate. She needs some. It is going to be a chocolate cake.

1. What is Susan going to do?
2. Ask questions with 'any'
   a) eggs   b) butter
   c) sugar   d) milk
3. What does she need? What hasn't she got? Why does she need it?
4. Ask "How much/many . . . is she going to use?"

3

This strike began last week and it is still going on. There are some policemen and strikers in front of the factory but only a few. It is Saturday and most of the men are watching a big football match. The strange thing is that there are not any reporters or television cameramen there; perhaps they are at the match too.

1. Ask questions with 'any'
   a) strikers   b) policemen
   c) T.V. cameramen   d) soldiers
2. Are there a few or quite a few people here?
3. Where are all the others?

4

Arthur ordered a steak with some salad and potatoes. The waiter brought him some salad with his steak a few seconds ago but he did not bring him any potatoes. Arthur is telling him to bring him some now. There are only a few people in the restaurant. Perhaps it is not very good.

1. Ask what Arthur ordered and what the waiter brought him!
2. What is Arthur telling him and why?
3. Ask how many people there are!

5

There are quite a few men in this pub. There are also a few women. It is almost closing-time (11 o'clock). The man looking at his wallet is called Fred Collins. He wants some more beer. The trouble is he has not got any money.

1. Ask questions with "Are there any . . . ?"
   or "Is there any . . . ?"
   a) men   b) women
   c) money in Fred's wallet
2. What is Fred doing and why?

(O'Neill, Kingsbury, Yeadon, and Scott 1971b: 27)

10   *Beauty isn't only skin deep*

The words also differ in the amount of dirt implied:

not very   very

←——————————————————————————————————————→

     dirty   **grimy**   **filthy**
                      grubby

	man	family	dog	house	windows	clothes	hands	face	streets	water	language	joke	mind	trick	business
dirty	+	+	+	+	+	+	+	+	+	+	+	+	+	+	+
filthy		+		+	+	+			+	+	+	+	+		
grimy		(+)	+	+	+	(+)	+								
grubby						+	+	+							

Notice that **dirty** and **filthy** are frequently employed figuratively to mean 'vulgar' or 'immoral'.

5 **Being attractive**

	making a pleasant impression on the senses	close to an ideal	worthy of being loved	suggest relative smallness	suggests femininity or delicacy	arousing interest	causing pleasure *or*	suggests lightness and grace	may suggest good manners	suggest sexual attraction	having well proportioned features	well made or of good quality	often suggests strength	often suggests dignity *or*	result of great generosity
beautiful	+	+													
lovely	+		+												
pretty	+			+	+										
charming	+				+	+	+								
attractive	+				+			+							
good looking	+								+						
handsome	+								+	+	+	+		+	

In this grid, *or* occurs alone in a box. It introduces a feature which is not in contrast with the one immediately before it. It is in contrast with an earlier feature presenting a basic sense. For example, [+ result of great generosity] is in contrast with [+ making a pleasant impression on the senses] and *not* with [+ often suggests dignity].

When qualifying people, **good-looking** and **handsome** are more often used for men, and **lovely**, **beautiful** and **pretty** for women. **Attractive** may be used for either. When qualifying inanimate and abstract nouns, there is often little semantic distinction between **beautiful**, **lovely**, **charming** and **attractive**.

(Rudzka, Channell, Putseys, and Ostyn, 1981: 10)

Other resources for language learning: As well as printed teaching materials—most commonly the textbook—teachers and learners may also have access to a range of resources such as the language laboratory, video, audio cassettes, film, etc.

► TASK 44

What can these alternative media contribute to the language learning process and what do they imply for the teacher's role?

1 Does the use of these materials improve motivation?

2 Could such resources ever replace teachers?

3 Does the use of such resources imply laziness on the part of the teacher?

4 Do these media supply alternative information about the nature of the target language and, as such, enrich the learning process?

5 Is the teacher's instructional role belittled by the use of these materials?

6 What sorts of role do these resources give to learners? Do learners, for example, sit passively and 'watch the video', or do they take an active part in interpreting what they see or hear?

7 What are the implications of the latter for the types of task learners perform with resources such as the video, tape recorders, and even the language laboratory?

Much depends on

1 the focus of the material—content or meaning
2 the types of activity we devise
3 the role of both teachers and learners when working with these materials

All these questions place in sharper relief the roles of teachers and learners. Is the teacher the operator of the on/off switch or is he an active participant in the process of making meaning out of the material, working with the learners?

4 Language learning tasks and activities

In order to find out about language learning tasks and activities, we need to address several important questions.

Is it sufficient to state baldly that 'teachers teach and learners learn'?
What do learners actually do in the classroom that marks their role behaviour?
How far do learners' goals interlock with teachers' goals?
How much does learner role behaviour influence teacher role behaviour and in what ways?
How far and in what ways is classroom language learning a co-operative endeavour? How do the development and character of classroom activity reflect the co-operative nature of the endeavour?

4.1 Learning groups and learning activities

► TASK 45

Consider the following quotes and their implications for language teaching.

1 It is all too easy for a foreign language classroom to create inhibitions and anxiety. It is not uncommon to find a teaching situation where, for example:
- the learners remain constantly aware of their own state of ignorance before a teacher who possesses all relevant knowledge
- they are expected to speak or act only in response to immediate stimuli or instructions from the teacher (or tape etc.)
- whatever they say or do is scrutinised in detail, with every shortcoming being made a focus for comment.
(Littlewood 1981: 93)

2 ... in order to use these techniques successfully there may have to be a radical change in the relationship between teacher and student. The activities cannot work unless there is a relaxed atmosphere. Rearranging the layout of the room will help, but you will also need to alter their idea, and possibly yours, of what the teacher is there for.
(Maley and Duff 1978: 17)

3 The principle of self-correction in groups may be modified
  in a number of ways to give variety to the process. With
  certain sorts of remedial work, or very elementary
  exercises, rapid individual self-correction from an answer
  card may be appropriate, especially if followed by brief
  discussion in twos and threes.
  (Brumfit 1980: 11)

4 ... it can hardly be claimed that the teacher stimulates
  communication between the members of the group: in fact,
  his presence alone is enough to short-circuit it, because he
  is seen as a leader and because the learners keep turning to
  him.

  To free himself from this role, the teacher can either use a
  large number of authentic materials as 'informants' or he
  can arrange for the participation of native speakers with
  whom the learners can practise under more realistic
  conditions.
  (Gremmo and Abé 1985: 240)

a. How far do these ideas take account of the nature of group
   processes?
b. Do you think they are realistic in view of what you experience in
   your own day-to-day classroom practice?
c. If you applied the ideas in 3 and 4 to your everyday practice, what
   do you think would be the results? For the group and for yourself,
   the teacher?

Now look at the piece of teaching material which follows and
consider how you might use it to promote learning activity in pairs
or small groups.

[B] These are the answers to five questions that could be asked about the passage in Question A. Can you say what these questions might be? For example: *Because his wife laughed lightly into her pillow* could be an answer to the question *Why was the chemist furious all over again, when he got back to the bedroom?*

1 From the smell of whisky on his breath and the fact that he was swaying.
2 Because the chemist shouted so loudly.
3 Because he had kicked them across the room.
4 One under the wardrobe and the other behind the dressing-table.
5 No. She stayed in bed.

[C] The blank spaces in these sentences can be filled by only one of the words or groups that are shown in italics beneath them. Which one?

1 If I had known that that film was on last week, I —— it.
   would see   had seen   would have seen   might see
2 Your temperature has dropped, so you —— take that antibiotic.
   must not   need not   don't   should not have
3 It was unkind of you to say that. You really —— done so.
   should not   should not have   need not   must not
4 I do wish you —— so much.
   haven't smoked   aren't smoking   didn't smoke   don't smoke
5 It's getting rather late. It's time we ——
   are going   went   go   must go
6 As soon as Dick ——, tell him I want to see him.
   will arrive   is arriving   arrives   will have arrived
7 This is the third time we —— this film.
   have seen   had seen   used to see   are seeing
8 We have lived here ever since we ——.
   were married   had married   have married   were marrying
9 No wonder those plants are dying. They —— any water for ages!
   haven't had   haven't   hadn't had   hadn't
10 They —— last week.
   might arrive   ought to arrive   must arrive   must have arrived

(Millington-Ward 1972: 3)

The 'climate of the classroom'

The combination of the task-related and interpersonal dimensions of a learning activity (see 2.2) provides an objective means of looking at the climate of the classroom. We are all aware of the atmosphere or tone of a classroom when we enter it either as teacher, learner, or observer. We are able, intuitively, to say whether it is 'warm', 'active', 'lively', 'dull', 'threatening', and so on. In part our conclusions are the result of our observations of the sorts of activity that are going on in the classroom.

▶ ## TASK 46

How far do different language learning activities promote different classroom climates?

For example, a mini lecture could be regarded as both highly instrumental and non-interactive in terms of inter-student activity.

Now think about the activities below. In order to assist yourself, ask the following questions:

1 Is the activity focused on either the teacher or the materials, or could it lead to collective participation by learners?

2 Is the object of the activity for learners to share their experiences and values or is it aimed at the learning or acquisition of facts?

3 Is a definite outcome, i.e. correct answer or answers, generated by the activity?

Explanation of grammatical rule
Role play
Project work
Simulation
Self-access work in the language laboratory
Free group discussion
Question and answer
Seminar
Computer-assisted language-learning programme
Structure practice drill
Guided writing exercise
Drama activities

Closed and open-ended activities

With many language learning activities, there is a definite outcome – a correct answer. Much of the time in the activity in the classroom is directed towards arriving at the desired outcome. As we saw, the answer is usually held by the teacher in view of his superior knowledge of the target language. Such activities might be described as *closed*.

In varying degrees there are other activities which can lead to more and more open-ended outcomes. There is no one correct answer or its equivalent. Such activities are *open*. Learners have more control over the latter type of activity and are much freer to reach their own conclusions in their own time. In fact time limits may become a major obstacle from the teacher's point of view, especially when the particular lesson has definite learning objectives in content terms.

Consider the following scenario:
A teacher takes the decision to introduce an activity into the classroom that best suits the learners' interests as he sees them. So he decides to base a lesson on pop songs ('my 15-year-olds are bound to like them') and the learners' reactions to them. Conflict is the outcome.

Do the learners feel that the teacher is patronizing them?
Do they feel cheated because that is not a normal language learning activity with a definite outcome?
Do they see the teacher as a weak leader, afraid to plough on with the curriculum, which is seen as 'learning language'—not songs?
What do you think? What would you do?

▶ **TASK 47**

Now consider each of the activities which follow in terms of the amount of control the learner might have over its organization and management in the classroom.

Can the learner decide what the topic or subject matter is?
Can the learner do the activity at his/her own pace?
Can the learner stop the activity at any time?
Is the activity open-ended in terms of its outcome?

Work on your own first. Then compare what you've done with your partner(s).
1 Is this young man looking directly at anyone or anything? Does his expression tell you what he is feeling? (Try covering the background with your hand in order to concentrate on his face.) Has he just been moving? Is he likely to move soon?
2 Now compare him with the others in the background. Is he in any way different? (Clothes? Expression?) Does he 'belong' here? Where is he? What is he doing here?
3 If this was a picture at a photography exhibition, what title would you give it? If it was an illustration to an article, what would be the title of the article? If it was a poster, what would be the text on the poster?

(Maley, Duff, and Grellet 1980: 8)

 3 Being a successful student

Work with a friend. Look at the questionnaire. Ask and answer.

> ### QUESTIONNAIRE
> 1 Have you got
>   a a good dictionary?   b a good reference grammar?
> 2 Do you keep a vocabulary book?
>   If so, how do you organise it?
>   a alphabetically
>   b under topics
>   c day by day, like a diary
> 3 How do you practise English outside the classroom?
> 4 What do you read in English as well as your classbooks?
> 5 How much time do you spend on your English homework every week?
> 6 Which do you find most difficult in English?
>   a listening   b speaking   c reading   d writing

(Hedge and Dobinson 1982:12)

The social climate of the classroom is, to a large extent, a result of a combination of the level and quality of the learners' involvement. This shows itself both in single activities, but also in lessons and over longer periods of time as well. Learning groups develop and change over time; the longer the group is together, the more opportunity there is for change to take place.

Interpersonal relationships between the participants develop and change as the group develops. The types of task and activity the group is engaged in will also affect these changes.

An analysis of this process might profitably begin by asking: to what extent do the activities we employ in the classroom lead to the sharing of personal experiences and values among the learners and between teachers and learners? The relevance and implications of this question are many and significant. For example, consider the following extracts:

1. *The content of the language lesson should be the student.* This might be phrased another way to focus more directly on the task of the teacher and that is, 'The job of the teacher is to work on the student, while the student works on the language'.
   (Spaventa 1980: 12)

2. In *Quartet 1* the activities are almost entirely based on cooperation between pairs or groups of individuals. Through the careful preparation for access to the texts, an attempt has been made to instil confidence, and this is reinforced by the non-judgemental attitudes engendered in the pair and group work.
   (Grellet, Maley, and Welsing 1982: 8)

3. . . . developing control of the use of language involves the student in doing things, in making choices, evaluating feedback, bridging information gaps. Such activities demand an environment where doing things is possible. Sitting in regimented rows under the eagle eye of a magisterial teacher, addressing all remarks to or through the teacher—this is a scene which destroys all hope of communication.
   (Johnson and Morrow 1981: 64)

By increasing the amount and quality of learner involvement in our classrooms, we are challenging commonly held beliefs about the teaching and learning process, in particular, those regarding the roles of teachers and learners. In order to maintain the equilibrium of the interlocking roles of teacher and learner, the following have to occur if the teacher reduces the level of his own involvement:

1 Learners will have to take some leadership decisions.
2 Learners will have to take management decisions relating both to the conduct of activities and the organization of their own learning.

3 Teachers and learners will have to cope with a new set of social relationships in the class.
4 Teachers will have to instruct less.

There are other effects to examine, but this fundamental realignment of teacher and learner roles must be seen against the background of

group expectations and norms
group and individual goals
leadership and friendship patterns within the group

▶ TASK 48

What do you think would be the effects of the changes outlined above on norms of behaviour in your class or society? Would they be considered as part of normal everyday behaviour or would they be seen as threats or interruptions to the normal run of events?

1 Individual learners are called upon to reveal personal information known only to themselves. Example:

III.9   Things I wish I'd known at 18

GRAMMAR: I do wish I'd ... , If only I'd ... , I wish I'd ...
LEVEL: Intermediate
TIME: 15–20 minutes
MATERIALS: None

In class

1 Write up these sentences written by the best-selling novelist, Catherine Cookson, about her teens:
I do wish I'd known more about sex – at that age I still thought that babies came through kissing.
I wish I'd known in those early days that I had the ability to draw.
Oh, if only I'd had an education at that age!

2 Ask the students to pick an age in their past and write five sentences expressing their regrets about that time:
I wish ...
If only ...
I do wish ...

3 Put the students in threes to compare regrets.

(Rinvolucri 1984:112)

2 Learners are asked to take responsibility for their own work
  schedules, both in class and for homework or private study.
  Example:

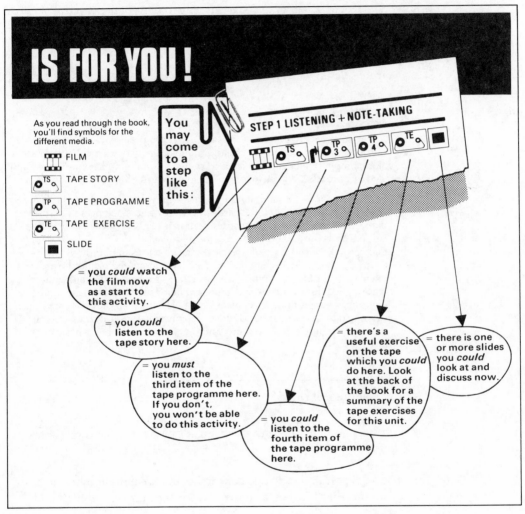

(Abbs, Candlin, Edelhoff, Moston, and Sexton 1982: i)

3 Learners are asked to work on open-ended tasks in small groups.

6.5   The rules of good taste

Work in groups of four or five. Can you agree on a set of five basic rules of good taste:

a) for decorating a house?
b) for how to dress?

Compare your list with the criteria of other groups.

6.6   Colours

Does everyone react to colour in the same way? Do preferences for one colour or another reflect a person's psychological make-up? Does the value attributed to colour simply reflect cultural rules? Try one of these simple experiments and see if you can reach any conclusions. Work in groups of four or five.

a) Each group makes a set of coloured cards: grey, blue, green, red, yellow, violet, brown, black. Lay the cards out one by one. Each person describes the feelings that the colour arouses in him or her. Contrasts between the colours and combinations can also be discussed.
b) Each group collects a set of postcard reproductions of paintings, each with a strong single colour element. The cards are circulated round the group. Each student notes down his or her reactions to the colours in the paintings, ignoring for the moment the compositional or thematic elements of the painting. There is no discussion at this stage. When all the cards have been examined by every member of the group, impressions are compared. The relationship between the colours and the themes of the paintings can also be examined.

(Porter Ladousse 1983:38)

4 Teachers join in an activity being done by the learners. For example:

> The teacher [. . .] has to decide whether to join in the activity as an equal member [. . .] or to remain in the background to help and observe.
> (Klippel 1984: 8–9)

5 Learners are asked to change the way in which they address their teacher (e.g. from 'Sir' to the teacher's first name).

How much is the classroom climate likely to be changed by these courses of action?

Would the changes be positive, negative or relatively neutral?

Would there be conflict? If so, between whom; teachers or learners?

Problems arising from each of the above scenarios might all be linked to conflicts with existing norms of behaviour.

If learners are asked to reveal personal information, they or their peers might well object. There may be social conventions which proscribe such revelations. Their expectations of either neutral or topic-loaded lesson content will be disappointed.

You might agree with the following writer's opinion.

> . . . I feel that probing too readily into the personal feelings of the learner becomes impertinent. The teacher-student relationship is unavoidably asymmetrical. However kindly, well meaning and democratic the teacher, the learner has less liberty to reject overtures than the teacher has, and the teacher should not presume upon the relationship: the learners must be free to decide how deeply to participate.
> (Brumfit 1981: 64)

Making learners responsible for their own learning schedules in even a token manner could conflict with the expectation that teachers are responsible for this element of learning management.

Existing conventions regarding the level of formality might be flouted by a change in modes of address. Modes of instruction are subject to expectations like all the other aspects of classroom behaviour. The expectation may be for teacher-led and dominated classroom activities.

The fact that conflict is possible reinforces the notion that there are norms and routines. Much depends on how much is taken for granted and what is assumed by teacher and learner.

▶ TASK 49

Examine the extract which follows:
> In terms of *content* [. . .] learners could be allowed choice in their reading matter.
> [. . .]
> In terms of *time* and *goals*, a lot more use could be made of project work. Learners could be required to devise their own project work in consultation with the teacher and to submit the completed work by some agreed date. How much time was spent working on the project, and when, could thus be left up to the learners.
> (Littlejohn 1985: 256)

What assumptions is the author making about the nature of group processes in the classroom?
What are the implications of this approach for the teacher?

What risks does the teacher run?

What are the major disadvantages of such an approach from the teacher's point of view?

What new skills might teachers have to develop?

Is it worth trying? Or is it simply impossible in certain social and cultural circumstances?

What are the implications of this approach for the learner?

Could the approach be used with any group, or would it only suit particular groups?

What sorts of skills might learners develop?

Cohesiveness and friendship in the group

In any learning group, patterns of friendship develop based on, for example, shared interests, mutual respect, and common background. Within the group, there also develop sub-groups who share these common bonds. This is neither unusual nor new. What is of interest, however, is the likely effect on these groupings of the introduction of new patterns of work in the classroom. Existing patterns of friendship must be taken into account when the teacher sets up small working groups.

Is it desirable, for instance, to form groups on the basis of friendship ties within the learning group? Does the present social climate of the group make it possible to break up sub-groups for the purposes of learning activities?

Does the teacher form the groups on the basis of ability or should the groups be formed on the basis of mixed ability?

What will be the effect across the whole class's friendship patterns and cohesiveness if the teacher withdraws from centre stage? Will new communication patterns emerge?

What are the implications for control, discipline, and efficiency of a withdrawal from centre stage by the teacher?

Communication patterns

Examine the diagrams which follow. Do you notice any similarities between the networks in these diagrams and the networks of small groups that we studied in Section One?

1 Teacher at centre stage

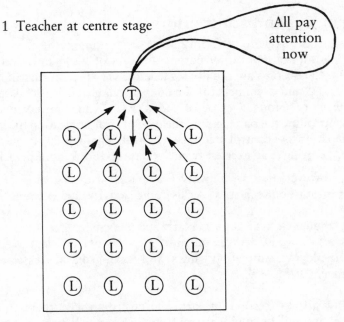

Figure 14

2 Teacher withdraws from centre stage

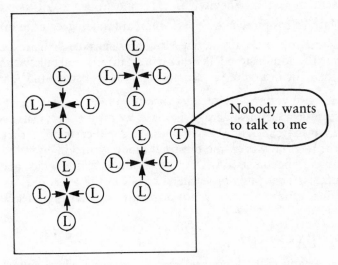

Figure 15

What are the possibilities for individual learners receiving individual attention from the teacher in the scenarios outlined above?

Communication patterns: formal or informal?

If a decision to change to different modes of working in the classroom is made, it has implications for the pattern and type of communication in the classroom. Classrooms are usually regarded as very formal environments, status-marked and asymmetrical. Lessons are likely to be 'focused' (see *Management of knowledge*) or of the 'Cook's Tour' variety with the teacher controlling the patterns and the type of communication. If, for any reason, teachers lose control of lessons, they can regain the initiative by, for example, reverting to an exercise from the class textbook, done in lockstep.

Assume, however, that we introduce activities with a greater affective involvement into our schemes of classroom activity, for example:

> A language class is a particularly suitable environment for meeting affective needs, because much of the activity can take the form of role-playing, simulation games, and small-group discussions. (Rivers 1981: 89)

If we allow greater freedom of participation from the learners, it is very likely that there will be a tendency for the classroom to become less formal.

Goffman (1981) notes that informal talk has the following characteristics:

1 There is a great deal more 'self-reporting', i.e. speakers are likely to reveal more about themselves and be more open to criticism from others.

2 Margins for error and imperfection are much greater in informal talk.

3 Correction is usually noticed by other speakers/listeners, but is rarely actually administered. In other words, in informal talk, we rarely correct others, or if we do, we usually signal it and stress the correction.

These observations are of relevance to language learning. If we allow a more informal atmosphere in the class, we must expect learners to be more ready to share meanings and values. This will certainly enrich the content of learning. However, the informal mode is also likely to be more risky because of the likelihood of imperfections occurring which may be noticed by others. The status of learners' errors in the L2 is thus unclear in the informal mode, where it is not normal to correct imperfections.

▶ ## TASK 50

Examine the language learning material which follows and comment on the likely outcome in terms of formal and informal talk.

What teacher and learner roles are implied in the material? Could you foresee different ways of using the material from those outlined by its author?

Unit 7
Things that have happened

A Have you ever...?

1 Listen to the song. You will hear it twice. The second time, try to remember the words that have been left out.

2 Ask and answer questions beginning *Have you ever eaten / seen / climbed / met / been to / broken /...?* etc.
Example:

HAVE YOU EVER EATEN OCTOPUS?

NO, I NEVER HAVE.

YES. I EAT IT EVERY DAY.

NO, BUT I'VE EATEN SHARK.

YES, I ATE SOME LAST SUMMER.

YES, I'VE EATEN IT TWICE.

3 Match the words and the pictures. Then ask and answer questions beginning *Do you ever...?* or *When you were a child, did you ever...?* Examples:

'Do you ever go walking in the rain?'
'When you were a child, did you ever go camping?'

1. refuse to take medicine
2. stay up all night reading
3. dream of being someone else
4. take part in demonstrations
5. go out alone
6. want to be taller or shorter

(Swan and Walter 1985: 30–1)

Unit 7: Lesson A

Students learn ways of talking about people's experience and habits.
Principal structures: revision of present perfect simple tense; present, past and present perfect with *ever; I've been to ...*
Words and expressions to learn: *song; job; ankle; billion; boat; dollar; grammar; ice-cream; advertisement; climb; go camping; run away; fight; past* (adjective); *in hospital; recently; on one occasion.*

Language notes and possible problems
1. Present perfect tense   The rules for the use of the present perfect are complicated. Here, students revise the use of the present perfect simple for *finished actions* in *unfinished time periods*: 'time up to now'.
Example: *I've eaten octopus twice (**in my life**).*
At the same time, students are reminded that they cannot use the present perfect tense with adverbs or other expressions which refer to a *finished* time period. Look out for mistakes like **I have had a car accident last year.*

The present perfect progressive, and some other uses of the simple tense, are studied in Lesson 7B.
2. Past participles   Some students may be unclear about the difference between simple past forms and past participles.

If you are short of time
Leave Exercise 9 for homework and drop Exercise 10.

1 Song
• The song is recorded twice – a complete version is followed by a gapped version.
• Play the complete version through once, while the students listen with their books closed.
• Ask what they have understood, and write on the board any words and phrases that they can recall.
• Play the complete version again, and see if students can recall any more.
• If they have found it easy to understand the song, go straight on to the gapped version. Play this once or twice, while students try to say or sing the words that go in the gaps.
• If this is too difficult, tell students that they can find the words of the song on page 156.
• Go through the text with them explaining any difficulties.
• Then tell them to close their books again, and try the gapped version.

2 Have you ever ...?
• Look at the example question with the students. Make sure they understand the meaning of *ever* with the present perfect (= at any time in your life).
• Go over the answers and explain any difficulties.
• Point out that the answer *Yes, I ate some last summer* is in the simple past tense because there is an adverbial of finished time (*last summer*).
• Ask students if they can think of other examples of this sort of adverbial.

• Get a few students to ask others if they have ever eaten octopus; make sure the tenses in the answers are correct.
• Then get students to ask each other more questions beginning *Have you ever ...?*
• You may wish to say a word about the use of *been* as a past participle of *go*, meaning *gone and come back*.

Optional activity   Survey
• Ask each student to prepare a question beginning *Have you ever ...?*
• Get everybody to stand up and walk round asking their questions and noting the answers.
• Then get students to report the results of their survey (e.g. *Seven people out of twelve have had piano lessons*; *Nobody has been to Australia*).
• (Note: this can also be done after Exercise 3.)

Optional activity   Question-box
• Ask students to prepare at least two questions beginning *Have you ever ...?*
• They must write their questions on separate pieces of paper, fold them up and put them in a box.
• The box is then passed round. Each student draws out a question, opens it, reads it aloud and answers.
• Tell students that they do not have to tell the truth if they don't want to. They can also reject one question, saying *I'd rather not answer* (put this on the board); but they are not allowed to reject two.
• When students have answered their questions, make sure they don't put them back in the box.
• (This activity can also be done after Exercise 3.)

3 *Do you ever ...?* and *Did you ever ...?*
• Give the students a minute or two to match the words and the pictures.
• Help with new vocabulary, and practise the pronunciation of the phrases.
• Then help them to practise the two example questions, paying attention to correct stress.
• Finally, get students to ask each other more questions in the simple present or simple past. They can use the phrases in the illustration or make up their own.
• This can be done in small groups, with each person asking the others at least two questions.

Optional activities
• If you have not already used the 'survey' or 'question-box' activity, these can be done now, using *Do/did you ever ...?*

(Swan and Walter 1985: 30–1)

4.2 The individual learner

The social climate of the classroom depends to a great extent on the strength of each individual's contribution. As a counterpoint to our discussion of the role of the learner in the context of group activity let us now examine it from the point of view of the individual learner.

Despite the tendency towards establishing group norms of behaviour in the classroom, every learner remains an individual; no learning group is ever totally homogenous except in cases of shared culture or roughly compatible age ranges. Even within such a group there is likely to be a series of differences between the individual learners.

Personality

We have examined personality traits in terms of teachers (see 1.2) and very similar observations could be made about learners' personalities. However, let us look at a scheme for studying the behaviour of individual learners based on actual observation of classroom interaction rather than psychological theory.

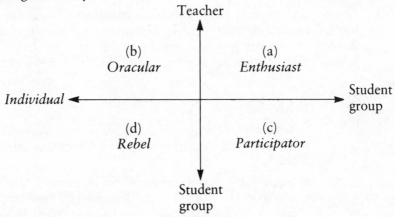

Figure 16 (after McLeish 1973)

Four main types of learner are distinguished in this analysis. Bearing in mind that individuals could be placed anywhere on this diagram and thus can differ according to the degree of the tendency towards being of any one type, the types are as follows:

1 The *enthusiast*—this type tends towards the teacher as a point of reference but at the same time is concerned with the goals of the learning group.

2 The *oracular*—again centres on the teacher but this time is much more oriented towards the satisfaction of personal goals.

3 The *participator* focuses attention both on group goals and on group solidarity.

4 The *rebel* leans towards the learning group for his or her point of reference but is mainly concerned with the satisfaction of his own goals.

► ## TASK 51

1 What are the implications of this categorization for the organization of learning groups in the classroom?

2 Which learners are more likely to respond to a teacher-centred approach?

3 Is it possible to influence changes in the behaviour patterns of different individual learners? Are these behaviours only exhibited in the learning situation or are they extensions of behaviour exhibited outside the classroom?

4 What is the relevance of these categories to the ideas you have on learner motivation and learners' needs?

Stages of development: personal and cognitive

In any learning group the members are at different stages of personal and intellectual development (see 2.1). The description of learner development in Section One may give us insights into the 'slow' or 'awkward' student who is stuck at stage 1, seeing the world in 'black and white'.

► ## TASK 52

1 What are the implications of individual differences in levels of personal and cognitive development for language learning and teaching?

2 Could learners who see the world in terms of 'black and white' be expected to cope with the demands of a view of language that sees communication as being indeterminate, negotiable, and ultimately risky?

3 Could learners at the 'black and white' stage honestly be expected to take responsibility for their own learning?

4 Would learners have to be assisted to move from the 'black and white' stage to the 'everything is relative' stage? What types of activity might assist learners in achieving this?

5 Does the scheme accord with various levels of language learner proficiency—intermediate, etc.?

6 Could the achievement of the 'commitment' stage be regarded as a legitimate goal of language study?

7 Do you think that the stages of development are applicable to the cultural group that you are working among? Or does the idea seem alien or foreign?

8 Is there a correspondence between the personality types of
learners and the stages of personal and intellectual development? Could it be, for instance, that the rebel personality is more
highly developed than the participator? What does this scenario
imply for teaching in predictable and rigid ways?

9 Is the answer a programme of learning for each individual? Or
could individuals select from the 'menu' what they feel is
appropriate for them as individuals depending on their stage of
development?

10 Does this, in fact, mean that the needs of the group must be
made subservient to the needs of the individual? Is a compromise
possible?

Learning styles and strategies

Learning style, which is to an extent observable, and learning strategy,
more a set of cognitive processes, are both key elements in the realization of
the learner's role. For example, the fact that learners ask questions is
enough evidence of their part in creating the learning process.

It is clear that there is a great deal we can learn from the examination of the
various strategies of the individual learner in managing her learning in the
course of language learning activities.

▶ TASK 53

Look at the list of language learning activities below.

Writing an essay
Doing a structure drill
Role play
Taking part in a simulation
Answering questions on a reading text
Making a summary of a listening text
Working out a grammatical rule from a set of examples
Free discussion
Teacher-led discussion
Project work
Learning a lexical set

For each of these activities answer the following questions:

1 Does the activity demand rote learning?
2 Does the activity demand original thinking?
3 Does the activity promote risk-taking?
4 Does the activity require inter-student communication?
5 Could the activity be performed by students working alone?
6 Does the activity encourage the learner to seek feedback from (a)
peers or (b) the teacher?

7 Does the activity encourage guessing?
8 Does the activity involve routines?

How do learners pursue their individual learning goals?
We must assume that learners regard it as a legitimate right to pursue individual learning goals in the classroom. Thus, anything that learners contribute or withhold from the classroom process is evidence that they are trying to pursue their individual learning goals and also to satisfy certain psychological needs. Learners accept or reject instruction in their general psychological atmosphere.

▶ **TASK 54**

Learners employ a variety of strategies, both cognitive and social, in the classroom. Examine the exchange between a teacher and a student and consider the possible explanations which follow it. Add your own if you can think of alternatives.

T   The present perfect, you see, links the past and the present . . .
S   But sir, you said earlier that . . .

Explanations—think of a context for each of them.

The student is challenging the teacher's authority.
The student wants clarification of the point.
The student has misheard what preceded.
The student is showing off to his classmates.

Now make a list of the information you would need to be in possession of in order to provide a full explanation of this exchange.

You can probably think of numerous other interpretations of this exchange. However, learners are far from passive in creating the classroom process, even in an environment dominated by the teacher.

For a full discussion of classroom interaction you could read Malamah-Thomas: *Classroom Interaction*, a companion volume in this series.

▶ **TASK 55**

Examine the examples of learning materials which follow and try to decide what sort of learning strategies might be promoted by each piece of material, e.g. guessing; sharing ideas with peers; memorization; risk-taking.

CURIOUSER AND CURIOUSER   47

Imagination: After each exercise you choose to do, get individual students or the students working in pairs or groups to verbalise their reactions for you and/or each other.

— Tell the students:

1. 'Imagine you are: changing a light bulb... now mime the action involved. Everyone work at the same time.' (Other examples can be: looking for a lost coin, hanging up a picture, wrapping a parcel.)

2. 'Imagine a jug of water is in front of you. Mime various ways of using it.' (eg. washing with it, putting goldfish in it, drinking it, watering plants.)

3. 'Imagine as you open a door that the room is full of: money... chairs... cobwebs... sausages ... people... books. Mime your reaction to this.'

4. 'Imagine and mime that you are walking on: ice... dry leaves... eggs... hot sand.'

5. 'Go into pairs. In pairs, you are A and B. A, draw something in the air with your finger. B, watch A, and when he or she has finished, copy his or her drawing in the air with your finger.' (The students work simultaneously.)

(Langenheim 1980: 47)

87 Brainstorming

Aims   *Skills* – speaking, writing
              Language – conditional, making suggestions
              Other – imagination, practice of important thinking skills
Level   Intermediate
Organisation Groups of four to seven students
Preparation None
Time   5–15 minutes
Procedure   *Step 1:* The class is divided into groups. Each group receives the same task. Possible tasks are:

(a) How many possible uses can you find for a paper clip (plastic bag/wooden coat hanger/teacup/pencil/sheet of typing paper/matchbox, etc.)?

(b) You have to make an important phone call but you have no change. How many ways can you find of getting the money for the call?

(c) How many ways can you find of opening a wine bottle without a corkscrew?

(d) How many ways can you find of having a cheap holiday?

The groups work on the task for a few minutes, collecting as many ideas as possible without commenting on them or evaluating them. *All* the ideas are written down by the group secretary.

Step 2: Each group reads out their list of ideas. The ideas are written on the board.

Step 3: The groups choose five ideas from the complete list (either the most original or the most practical ones) and rank them.

Variations 1: After Step 1 the groups exchange their lists of ideas. Each group ranks the ideas on its new list according to a common criterion, e.g. practicability, costs, simplicity, danger, etc.

2: Each group chooses an idea and discusses it according to the procedure in No. 89 *Consequences*.

Remarks   Brainstorming increases mental flexibility and encourages original thinking. It is a useful strategy for a great number of teaching situations.

(Klippel 1984: 96–7)

Activity 7   Study the following paragraph and then complete
                        the diagram after it.

CLASSIFICATION OF PLASTICS
The behaviour of plastics when heated provides
the basis for the distinction between the two main
classes of plastics available today. Those like
polythene, PVC, perspex and nylon, which soften
when heated and become rigid when cooled again,
are called thermoplastics; with further heating and
cooling these plastics can be made to change their
shape repeatedly—like the gramophone record.
This processing is possible because only weak
bonding is present between neighbouring molecules,
and when warm the molecules slide very easily
past one another. On the other hand, plastics which
become rigid on further heating and cannot be
softened again are called thermosetting plastics.
Examples are Bakelite and Melamine. These
materials consist of polymer chains which react
with one another at points of contact so that they
become strongly linked together in three dimensions. The intermolecular bonds then prevent
relative movement of the original chains—in fact
the material is really one single molecule.
From: C. W. A. Newey *The Plastics and Steel
Industries* in *The Man Made World* (Open University)—slightly shortened

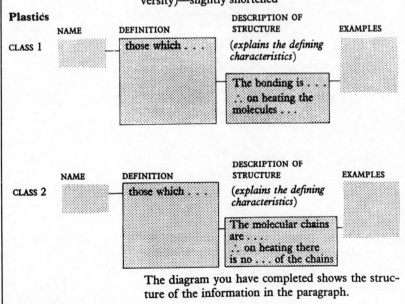

The diagram you have completed shows the structure of the information in the paragraph.

(Moore 1979: 82–3)

4.3 Classroom processes: summary

In this section we have tried to build up a framework within which to consider the classroom process from the differing perspectives of teachers and learners. Roles are played out in relation to the following factors:

1 *Goals* We have seen how goals affect the participants' interpretation of their roles.

2 *Tasks* We have seen how the type of task and its mediation in the classroom is a reflection of both goals and roles.

3 *Topics* We have seen the importance in the differing perspectives of participants towards both the subject matter of the language lesson and the way in which it is dealt with in the lesson.

> What aspects of the material presented in Section Two do you think you need more information on?
> Are there any notions which intrigue you and you would like to follow up in your own classroom situation?

Prepare a set of problem questions on any of the following:
learning materials
learning activities
learning modes and styles
teaching style
instructional modes

Investigating teacher and learner roles

Teachers' primary roles are instructional and managerial. Learners, too, have reciprocal managerial and learning roles. This final section is designed to assist both parties to develop and enhance the effectiveness of these roles. In order to achieve this from the teacher's point of view, a third major role is presented for your consideration: *investigator*.

This role is based on the following assumptions:

1 In order to develop as both a professional and an individual, a teacher can consider reflecting upon and evaluating his own experience. This can be done alone or with the assistance and support of colleagues and friends.

2 Teachers can become better teachers – more sensitive to the demands of their learners and better equipped to manage the learning process.

3 Learners can become better learners – more efficient at their task and also better able to participate in learning activities.

4 The total classroom process involving both teachers and learners can become better suited to the promotion of learning.

Consider this extract from a very influential work on language teaching:

> Our lack of certainty about how language is put to communicative use might incline us to the view that we should wait for more definitive findings to emerge from research before we adopt a communicative orientation to the teaching of language. I think this would be an unfortunate view to take. It would imply that language teachers are simply consumers of other people's products, that they are incapable of initiative and must only make advances in methodology across ground already prepared by proclaimed theorists. But the language teacher need not, and usually does not, assume such a passive role. He can, and does, conduct operational research and he is in the position of being able to explore the possibilities of a communicative approach to teaching for himself.
> (Widdowson 1978: 162–3)

This section of the book is concerned with tasks with which to investigate aspects of the teacher's and learner's role behaviour.

1 There are tasks to enable readers to find out about existing practices, to interpret the results and take action on the basis of their investigations.

2 Means will also be suggested in a further series of tasks as to how to investigate problems that teachers have identified for themselves. In short, there will be suggestions on how to go about what Widdowson terms 'operational research' in a systematic manner.

You might already have said to yourself things like, 'I want to understand what happens in my classroom', or, 'Things aren't going very well at present: what's going wrong?' These perceptions are a useful starting point for the use of this section of the book. It is intended that readers work on tasks that are of particular concern to them.

Whichever part of the section you do work on, it is advisable to follow the task instructions very carefully.

Preliminaries

1 Write down what you see as the main problems you have in your roles as manager and instructor of your learning group.

2 Decide whether your interests and problems are in the interpersonal or the task-related areas, or equally spread in both areas.

5   Some investigations

▶ ## TASK 56

Aim
To investigate 'classroom climate' and to see how it is influenced by the roles taken by teachers and learners.

Possible applications
To see if it is possible and/or desirable to introduce new working patterns into the classroom.

Procedure
1 Agree to work with one or more colleagues with the same aim.

2 Work out a schedule for observing each other's classes over a two-week period. Try to watch at least two of your colleagues' classes and have them do the same for you.

3 When you observe, tell the class what you are doing. Something like, 'I am watching this class at work to see if together we can devise new ways of teaching you. We also want to find out how you work together as a group.' This is important, otherwise the class may think that you are observing them in order to evaluate their performance and they will probably behave out of character.

4 While watching the class, sit in a position where you cannot be seen by the majority of the class.

5 Take notes under the following headings:

Seating arrangements during the lesson: Do they stay the same or are they varied? What is the effect of the seating arrangements on the atmosphere in the class?

Teacher/learner relationships: Are they warm or cold? Distant? Close? Does the teacher have time for individual consultation with the learners? Does this seem to have been planned?
Does the teacher opt for affiliative or dominant behaviour with the learners?
How does the teacher deal with any discipline problems that occur? What seems to cause these problems?

Types of learning task being worked on: Are they open or closed, or is a mixture used? If so, what sort of balance is there? Are the learners busy or bored?

Inter-student communication: Is this part of an activity, or does it happen in spite of the teacher's presence? Is it warm or cold?

When the class has finished, try to ask a small group of learners from the class what they felt the class was like.
Did they think they had enough time to do what they wanted in the lesson?
Did they feel that they had learnt much from the lesson?
Did they enjoy the lesson?
Did they feel they had enough chances to participate in the lesson?

6 As soon as possible after the lesson, get together with the teacher you are working with and discuss the lesson. Tell her what you observed; ask her if she feels the same way. Ask if this was a typical lesson with the group in question. Did anything out of the ordinary happen?

7 Have your colleague(s) repeat the procedure with one of your classes and go through steps 3–7.

8 At the end of the agreed period of observation, meet with your colleagues to interpret and evaluate what you have seen and recorded.

Interpretation and evaluation
When you meet with your colleague(s) to review the observation, try to establish possible reasons for the positive and negative features of the classes and to make constructive suggestions as to how to improve.
Note – similarities between the classes;
    – differences between the classes.
Try to isolate the influence of the seating arrangements, the types of learning task on the general atmosphere and also whether you think that these contribute to the quality of the teacher/student relationship.

Evaluate your own lesson and get your colleague(s) to evaluate their lessons with the following questionnaire: Mark yourself as follows: **A** (Good), **B** (Satisfactory), **C** (Moderate), **D** (Poor) on the following criteria:

> responsiveness to learner needs
> encouragement of learner self-discipline
> encouragement of learner participation
> appropriateness of materials or task
> management and organization of class
> overall classroom climate

Action
1 If you find that the seating arrangements had an inhibiting effect on any of the classes, experiment with alternative arrangements, as described in Section Two. Task 59 also shows how to go about this.

2 If you find that the learning tasks seemed to have a negative effect on the class's atmosphere, introduce new types of task into the teaching/learning sequence. Task 69 shows how to do this.

3 If a teacher seemed to be the cause of a negative atmosphere in any class, ask to observe or be observed again in order to try to establish some of the possible causes of the problem.

4 If you found that all the classes went well, draw up a list of ways of creating a warm atmosphere in the class. Other teachers may want to hear about these. Ways of distributing your results are discussed in 6.

▶ TASK 57

Aim
To find out preferred working patterns in a learning group.

Potential application
This is particularly valuable before setting up project groups as it will give you insights into potential conflicts between learners in the group.

Note: It is advisable to do this with a group of thirty or less as collating the results can be time-consuming with a large group.

Procedure
1 Tell the class what you are going to do. Tell them that you are going to find out who likes working with whom so that you can organize the class better for certain activities.

Note: All instructions for this task can be given to the learners in the mother tongue if this is appropriate.

2 Tell the class that what they write will not be seen by any person other than yourself.
3 Give each learner a blank piece of paper and tell them to write their name at the top.
4 Ask the learners to write the name of the person in the class they like working with best.
5 Then tell them to add, in rank order, as many of the other members of the class as they wish.
6 Now tell the class to turn their paper over and to write the names of those with whom they least like working, again in rank order, from least desired working partner.
7 When all the class has finished collect in the papers.

Interpretation
1 Begin by noting the most chosen learner and the names of those who choose him or her.
2 Next, add the names of learners who have made mutual choices.
3 Start a separate group for the next most popular learner, and so on. Again, add choices which are mutual.
4 Start to construct a diagram like the sociometry one below. (The names are fictitious). The arrows indicate: → likes and ----→ dislikes. Your final diagram will show the following:
   the most preferred members of the learning group for doing group tasks
   those who are isolated
   those who make mutual choices

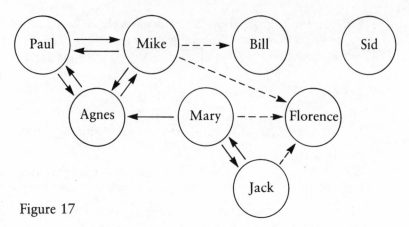

Figure 17

Action

1 You can use the diagram as the basis for a group discussion about preferred working partners, their qualities, and their strengths. It can also form the basis for a discussion about the qualities of friends and workmates and whether they differ. These discussions are best held in classes that know each other well and are likely to be frank and fair with each other.

2 You may, on the other hand, use the diagram as evidence for underlying conflicts between class members and use it to try to bring these differences into the open in the hope of clearing up the atmosphere. You are the best judge of how risky a course of action this may be.

3 You can use the diagram as the basis for organizing working groups. You must also observe these groups when they are at work in order to see if the patterns are verified in practice. Task 59 on classroom organization will give you some ideas on how to do this.

4 You can use the diagram as the basis of an investigation of the friendship groups in the class. It will be interesting to see if learners choose to sit by preferred working partners or not.

▶ **TASK 58**

Aim
To keep a record of classroom events as the basis for reflection and possible future action.

Possible applications
You may wish to investigate a particular issue or problem or to keep a record in order to diagnose problems and their causes. You may wish to use it as the basis for a self-evaluation of your own teaching techniques and their effect on the class or your own teaching style. Whatever the case, try to be objective!

Procedure

Plan to keep your lesson notes in an exercise book. Set out your notes on the left-hand page and leave the right-hand page for:

– keeping notes while teaching—note reactions to questioning techniques, approaches to tasks you set, seating arrangements, preferred working partners in group work if you employ the method, conflicts with and between learners. Note these opposite the relevant stages of your lessons;

– writing a brief evaluation of the lesson and your impressions and feeling about specific events or the lesson as a whole and how you think the roles you adopted influenced these events.

Write your notes and comments in the language you feel most at ease with.

Interpretation

Review your notes and comments.

How do you think your role influenced classroom events? How did you actually fulfil your role? How many times did you find yourself acting as an informant; giving information to learners; as a guide; helping them through a learning activity, and so on?

Look for trends such as an apparent falling off of motivation or a corresponding increase in motivation among the learners and yourself.

See, for example, if there are trends in the development of the learning group such as:

    group solidarity
    norms of behaviour
    preferred ways of working

See 2.3 for ideas on what to observe in this respect.

Share these reviews with colleagues if you are working with a group. A very productive strategy is for a group to keep diaries over a period of, say, one month, and to meet to share the material in an effort to solve collective problems. This is particularly useful if you share the teaching of a class with another colleague; it adds to the informal comments which you may pass in the teachers' room. Your point of departure for keeping a diary may come from one of these more informal observations. The diary *records* these often fleeting impressions.

Action

1 Your findings may give you ideas for precise features of classroom life to investigate. Go to 6.2 to plan your investigation.

2 You may feel confident enough in the learning group to introduce new materials or modes of working having seen their development over a period of weeks.

3 Continue keeping the diary if it is a source of reflection and security, as well as data on your groups' life in the classroom.

▶ TASK 59

Aim

To set up new modes of classroom organization and to evaluate their effects on learner roles.

Procedure

1 When you want to introduce a new working pattern in your class, you have to prepare the learners for the new pattern. Let's say you want to try group composition.

2 Give the learners the following questionnaire to assess their attitudes and expectations in advance of your experiment.

Do you prefer to work alone? Why?
In what ways is working alone easier?
In what ways is working with others easier?
What problems do you have when working with others?
Do you like to help others? How?
Do you like others to help you? In what ways?
Do you feel uncomfortable about asking for help? Why?
Do you feel uncomfortable about using others' ideas? Why?
(Adapted from Lemlich 1979: 49)

As a result of this survey you will be able to decide whether or not to proceed. The learners may not be ready for group work or self-directed learning and may need to be introduced to these modes at a later date.

If the response is, on the whole, positive, you can proceed to the next stages.

3 Form a demonstration group from the class. Seat them in full view of the rest of the class. Tell the rest of the class to watch what you and the group are doing.

4 Set a task similar to the one you want the class to do for the demonstration group. Join in with them and briefly guide the group through each stage of the task. The rest of the class watches this and asks any questions that they want to.

5 Divide the remainder of the class into groups and set them off on the task.

6 While they are working, observe the groups at work. Be prepared to assist if they are having difficulty with the procedure.

Features to note

Co-operation and conflict in the groups
Enjoyment or boredom
Speed of execution of the task
Leadership patterns in the groups

7 When the activity is finished, let the class make a brief evaluation of the activity. Try this one, using a questionnaire. Answer with *yes* or *no*.

a. Did you enjoy working with a small group?
b. Did you find that you learnt more working with a group?
c. Would you like to work this way again?
d. Do you think that the teacher gave you enough assistance and guidance during the activity?
e. Did you find it easy to decide what to do with your group?
f. Did you feel that one group member dominated the task?

Interpretation

Draw up a balance sheet of the positive and negative features of the activity and the way the groups worked on it. Depending on the feedback you get from the questionnaire and your own observations, you will be able to gauge whether or not to use the technique again.

Even if response is fairly muted or negative, a strategy to employ now is to observe a colleague using group organization in one of their classes. Use the same observation checklist.

If the response is good, try the technique again with a new activity as its basis. Remember that the activity may have been the source of difficulty.

Action

1 When you use the group work method for the second and subsequent times, start to observe the groups at work. Concentrate on one in particular in the first instance. Do not sit with them; sit at a reasonable distance and observe.

2 Note the following:
   - Whether or not there is a definite leader.
   - If there is a leader, does he or she dominate the exchanges or does he or she act as a collector of information?
   - Is the group focused on the learning task or are they more interested in chatting among themselves?
   - Are there arguments or discussions over procedure?
   - Does the group's communication pattern seem to conform to any of the patterns set up by Leavitt? (See Section One, 1.2.)

3 Repeat the pre- and post-activity questionnaires. Has there been an improvement in the class's attitude towards the working pattern?

4 In the next lesson, try to observe as many groups as you can on the guidelines suggested in 2 above.

5 Adjust tasks or seating arrangements, depending on what you see as posing particular problems for the groups you observe.

Note: A class will probably take time to adapt itself to new working modes. It is important that you monitor the process and evaluate it as often as possible. You may wish to record the development of the groups over time and keep a record. (See Task 57 for ideas on this.)

▶ **TASK 60**

Aim
To find out what a new group of learners expects of a teacher's role.

Possible application
To match teaching style and learning activities with learners' expectations.

Resources
You will need multicopies of the short questionnaire that follows and possibly a tape recorder if you want to record the feelings and opinions of some of the group for future reference.

Procedure
1 When you meet the class for the first time, tell them that before you start working together you want to know how they have been taught before and whether they liked it.

2 Distribute the questionnaire. Tell the learners not to write their name and that only you, the teacher, will actually see their responses.

QUESTIONNAIRE

Instructions to learners: please complete this questionnaire as honestly as you can. It is designed to find out how you have been taught before and how you like to be taught. Just circle your chosen reply: YES/NO/DON'T KNOW.

a. In your last school, did your English teacher always explain every point to you?   YES/NO/DON'T KNOW

b. Did your last English teacher ever ask you to work in groups or pairs on language problems or exercises?   YES/NO/DON'T KNOW

c. Did your last teacher ever ask you about the ways in which you like to learn?   YES/NO/DON'T KNOW

d. Did your English teacher usually stand at the front of the class when he/she was teaching?   YES/NO/DON'T KNOW

e. Did the teacher always use the textbook for teaching?   YES/NO/DON'T KNOW

f. Did you enjoy English classes at your last school?   YES/NO/DON'T KNOW

g. Did your English teacher ever ask you to decide what to do in English classes?   YES/NO/DON'T KNOW

3 If you have the equipment, record the feelings of three or four of the learners, chosen at random. Use the same questions but allow the learners to speak at length on each question.

Note: Both the questionnaire and the interviews can be administered in the learners' L1.

Interpretation
The questionnaire should give you a rough guide to expectations as to your role in the language classroom.

1 What sort of environment do you think learners who provide a high proportion of 'Yes' answers to questions **a, b, d, e,** and **f** have been used to?

2 What can you conclude from an affirmative answer to question **g**, a negative answer to question **f**, and an affirmative answer to question **c**?

Action
You will now know how quickly you can proceed to introduce new modes of learning and how to adjust your own role to meet with the learners' expectations. You will also know how much you will need to do to prepare the ground for changes.

▶ ## TASK 61

Aim
To observe the relationship between teaching method and learners' affective involvement in classes.

Resources
You may want to make tape recordings of the classes you observe for future reference. Remember that if the class has more than twenty-five students it is very difficult to keep track of who is speaking and also that people far from the tape recorder will be difficult to pick up on the recording.

Procedure
1 Either record one of your own classes or get the agreement of a colleague to record theirs or observe it. Features to note:

Level of enjoyment: Was there a lot of laughter? Who or what provoked the laughter – teacher's joke? a learner's comment or joke? something in the learning materials?

Postures of participants: Were they relaxed/ alert/ resigned? Did these change during the class? If so why? Was the change due to a change in activity, or because the teacher remarked on the way a learner or learners were sitting?

Inter-student communication: Did the teacher give permission because of the activity, or was it an integral part of the learning activity, i.e. group or pair work?

Learner activity: Were the learners active or passive? Was this due to activity or other factors? Was it related to the amount of time the teacher was talking?
Were the learners attentive at all times or were there periods of boredom and inattentiveness?

Type of activity: Was the activity open-ended or closed? What was the language focus: grammatical, functional, or another?
Was the task clearly presented? Was the task appropriate?

Discipline: Were learners well-behaved? Did the teacher ever have to reprimand them? Why did the teacher reprimand if he did? Was this related to any learning activity?

2 *Either*: interview the teacher you observed and get his impressions on what you noted
Or: write a brief evaluation of your own class using the categories for observation.

Interpretation
Listen to the tape recording or review your own notes and check:

Negative impressions: Too much of the teacher talking, not enough student activity?
Dull learning activities? Learning activities too complex for learners?
Negative attitudes of the learners towards the 'subject'?
Too difficult? Unimaginatively taught?
Class afraid of teacher and therefore do just as teacher says?

Postive impressions: Lively teacher – plenty of humour?
Interesting and challenging learning activities?
Plenty of co-operation between learners?
Positive attitude of learners? Very involved and interested?

Action
Change teaching style? How?
Introduce new activities into the class?
Introduce new subject matter or new approach to previously-studied material?
Experiment with new organizational patterns?

Reaction
Monitor changes with the diary method. (See Task 58.) Adjust the focus of organization of activities when it seems necessary.

▶ **TASK 62**

Aim
To observe the relationship between instructional style and teacher and learner role.

Resources
In order to focus more closely on the features outlined in the procedure below, you may decide to make a tape recording of the lesson you observe, whether it is your own or a colleague's.

If you do not have access to a tape recorder, it is best to limit your observations to one specific feature in the lesson you observe. You may decide to observe a series of lessons to observe each feature outlined below.

Procedure
Observe a colleague's lesson and later have the same colleague observe one of your lessons.

1 Decide to focus on one of the following:

The level of formality of the lesson: What proportion of the time does the teacher spend focusing; on 'Cook's Tours, on 'Freewheeling'?
Note the occurrence of these instructional styles and decide roughly how much of the lesson is devoted to each.

The number of times the teacher gives mini-lectures in explanation of points: Contrast this with the use of elicitation in the lesson.
What does the teacher use it for? When?

The way the teacher uses teaching materials: What does the teacher do with the materials? Does the teacher teach everything in the materials or is a selection made?
Are the materials used to support the lesson or do they seem to drive it?
Do the learners have a choice over what parts of the materials are used?
Are the materials open-ended, closed or a combination of the two?
Are the materials used to control the class or are they used to generate discussion, speculation or the exploration of attitudes and feelings?

2 Make notes on the events you observe.

3 After the class, interview the teacher and get his perceptions on what you have noted.
For example, if you chose to observe the way the teacher uses materials, ask the teacher what he or she thinks materials are used for—control, discussion, etc.

Interpretation

1 If you made a recording, make up a checklist using the ideas from the observation procedure. Listen to the recording, noting where there is an occurrence of a feature on the checklist. Put a tick (√) when a feature occurs.
Your checklist may look something like this:

    Focusing
    Cook's Tour
    Freewheeling
    Self-access
    Mini-lecture
    Elicitation
    Materials – teaches through
              teaches with
              promotes discussion
              promotes speculation
    Teacher role – dominant
              participatory
              guiding
              resource

Learner role – passive
        controlled by teacher
        controlled by task
        contributory
        involved in decision-making

2 Now assess the balance between the various categories. Is the lesson teacher- or learner-centred or does it vary according to the activity? Is the lesson content- or process-oriented?

3 Are there any obvious reasons for the teacher and learner roles that you have seen in action through the teacher's instructional style and the learners' ways of participating?
What are the implications? Could the situation be rectified?
Does it need to be changed? Do the learners seem to enjoy the instructional style you have observed?

Action
1 Try different ways of organizing your lessons from the point of view of instruction. For example, instead of lecturing, try to elicit more.
Ask a colleague to observe you or record yourself teaching.
When you listen to the recording or do the observation, make a note of the following features:

    Space allowed for learner responses to questions
    Time allowed for learners to guess answers
    Willingness of teacher to provide answers to questions
    Learner response to elicitation – positive or negative?

2 See what the effect of using different types of task is on the learners and your own teaching. Make sure that you monitor this. (See Tasks 57, 58, and 62 for ways in which to do this.)

3 Try giving the learners more say in the ways in which they work and the types of materials they use.

4 Find out what the learners' preferred mode of instruction is. (See Tasks 59 and 63.)

Reaction
Repeat the investigation after a reasonable period of time has elapsed, say one month. Note any changes and the effects of the changes. Reinterpret as above. Try new courses of action not already taken.

► **TASK 63**

Aim
To observe learner strategy in classroom language learning activities.

Procedure
A with your own class
1 Set a task which has to be solved by the learners working in small groups.

2 Arrange the learners into their groups and set up the task or activity.

3 Observe one group at work. Make up a table with the students' names along one side and your observational categories on the other. (Tick (√) for each time a student acts in the ways listed.)

	Paul	George	John	Richard	etc
Guessing the meaning of a word					
Guessing grammatical rules					
Questioning another group member's contribution					
Deliberate time-wasting or obstruction of the process					
Provoking conflict					
Speculating on the answer to a question					

Figure 18

B with a colleague's class

Either repeat the procedure in **A** *or* watch the whole class and note the same phenomena.

Interpretation

1 Identify the main learner strategies in your sample.

2 Ask yourself these questions:
   What does this imply for the learners' role in the activity you observed?
   Does this accord with their own perceptions? (Interview learners to crosscheck.)
   Which is the most prevalent strategy: cognitive or affective?

3 Decide on explanations for the prevalent learner role that you observed.
   Was it related to the task?
   Was it related to the mix of personalities in the group?
   Was it related to the teacher's managerial or instructional style?
   Any other explanation?

Action

Depending on the answers to question 3 above, and on your assessment of the learners' preferences for learning strategies, you might consider:

   a. varying the tasks so that learners can have more opportunities to make guesses or speculate;
   b. reducing your own talking time to allow for learners developing their own strategies;
   c. changing the mix of learners working in the groups.

Reaction
Follow the same procedure again after any changes have been made. This time, allow the learners to contribute to the investigation by soliciting their opinions and perceptions on their strategies.

Give them a questionnaire and ask them to answer using *yes* or *no*.

a. Do you like to guess meanings of words or grammatical rules?
b. Do you like taking part in activities which invite you to solve a problem or speculate on the situations which are described?
c. Do you think you have enough opportunities to develop your learning strategies at your own pace and in your own time?
d. Do you think that you get enough opportunities to ask questions about points that confuse you and points that you want to know more about?
e. Do you ever find that the lesson or activity is proceeding too quickly or slowly for you?

Collate the answers you have received from the questionnaire and again make adjustments to the learning activities or your own instructional strategies.

▶ TASK 64

Aim
To observe learner style in order to establish a relationship between it and learning activity.

Procedure
1 Draw up a list of the members of your class and try to categorize each one in terms of the characteristics outlined under *Individual learners* in Section Two, i.e. *oracular*, *participator*, etc.
2 Have a colleague observe you teaching and ask him or her to give his or her own judgement of the learners in the class.
3 Compare your judgements and draw up a final list.
4 Have your colleague observe and note the participation patterns of the learners. He or she must also note changes in these patterns in all classroom activities and whether or not they are related to the activities that the class is doing, and also your role as the teacher.
5 Repeat the procedure with your colleague's class.

Interpretation
What conclusions can you draw from the observation? Do certain types of activity or instructional style seem to favour certain learners at the expense of others? What are these activities or instructional styles?
Do certain learners seem to be at a disadvantage with certain types of instructional style?

Action

Do you need to vary the types of task and activity to promote certain learner types?

Do you need to adjust your instructional style to cater for all the learners in your group?

Reaction

Repeat the procedure over a longer period, say, one academic term, to establish the correctness of your original categorization and also to note changes in students' behaviour. Are the changes due to changes in instructional type or are they due to other factors?

▶ TASK 65

Aim

To set learning objectives with your learning group.

Procedure

1 Collect as much information as you can about the language learning curriculum of your group. This may include copies of national, school and course syllabuses, as well as course materials which are prescribed and ways of evaluating their learning such as progress tests and samples of public examination papers if necessary.

2 Present the students with the following categories. They can be put as headings on large wallcharts which will be filled in after the activity in below or alternatively as headings on the blackboard.

   Objectives: What do you want to achieve?

   Evaluation: How do you want to be evaluated?

   Working modes: How would you like to work in the class—with your friends or with the teacher leading class activities?

   Activities: What sorts of activity and language learning activity do you want to do?

   Materials: What sorts of learning material would you like to work with? Textbooks/ Newspapers and books in English/ Magazines/ Tape recordings of native English speakers.

3 Furnish the learning group with samples or summaries of the 'official' learning objectives. Either give this as a handout or put it on the wall.

4 Tell the learners their task is to record 'what to do this week/month' by answering the main questions set out in 2 above.

Action

Set up a system for learners to do the following:

   1 Evaluate activities they do (see Task 59 and also Task 68).
   2 Set realistic learning objectives and goals.
   3 Choose their working modes.

4 Choose learning materials.
5 Choose the activities they want to do.

Set up a parallel system for you to monitor the work that the students do.
This is best achieved by the learners keeping a record of what they do and also 'publishing' aspects of what they do.
See the sample record and objectives sheet below from Dan (1983):

Please complete this sheet regularly			
Name:			
Subject/Aims:			
Date	Task/Activity	Materials	Comments
Homework/Extra study:			
Teacher's comments:			

Figure 19

Reaction
Adjust learner involvement if the learners are finding difficulty in setting objectives. Give them assistance and guidance based on past performance, for example:

provide more learning materials if the learners are having difficulty in making choices, or provide more latitude for choice;
allow for variable working modes—individual, group, pairing in the learning group.

▶ TASK 66

Aim

To evaluate existing or new learning materials for indications of teacher and learner role.

Procedure

1 Examine the learning materials with reference to the checklist below. Put a tick (√) if the material has the feature indicated.

> Clear instructions to learners as to the working mode to be adopted for each exercise, task, or activity in the material.
> Clear choice of ways to go through the materials.
> Clear statement of the types and purposes of language the learners are working for.
> Clear indications as to the role teachers are supposed to fulfil in each task etc.
> Potential for adaptation of the materials to other working modes.
> Potential in the materials for speculation, discussion, or argument among learners.
> Definite outcomes to the activities in terms of right or wrong answers.
> Variety of task or exercise types.
> Means of evaluating teacher and learner contributions and performance.

2 Give the learners the following questionnaire:

> What do you think are the most useful ways of learning a new language?
> What do you think are the best types of language learning activities and tasks? Give reasons.
> What do you expect a teacher to do to help you when you are learning a new language?
> What can learning materials best provide you with when you're learning a new language?
> What do you think are the best kinds of language learning materials? Why?

> (Adapted from Breen and Candlin 1987)

Interpretation

On the basis of your survey, you will be able to come to some conclusions about the open-endedness or closed nature of the material and the potential for adopting a scheme of self-paced learning or a variety of learning modes for the learners. If there is a clear indication of the type of language study the materials are aiming for then you may be able to assist learners in coming to conclusions about their own learning objectives.

Action

1 Adapt the material for different working modes.

> For example, a blank-filling structure exercise (see Task 45) can be the

basis of interesting and productive group or pair work if groups of learners are instructed to identify correct answers and to speculate on the reasons for the incorrectness of the other alternatives in a multiple choice exercise.

2 Use the contents page of a textbook in the following way:

distribute it to the learners and ask them to choose what they think are the most important items to study;

ask the class to identify material, especially grammar points, which they have done before. Use their opinions as the basis for your own or their scheme of work.

3 Closely monitor the use of new material to see how it involves learners in sharing information and opinions, as well as working co-operatively (see Task 58, for example).

Reaction

Ask for learners' opinions and reactions to the materials. (See Task 68.) Monitor the use of the materials with several groups of learners and adapt them according to the outcomes that you desire in terms of group processes and a more flexible learner role in your class.

▶ ## TASK 67

Aim

To find out what teachers' books for either existing or new materials say about teacher and learner role.

Procedure

Go through the teacher's book with the following questions in mind.

  a. Is there any mention of teacher and learner role in the teacher's book?
  b. What sorts of role does the teacher's book give to teachers and learners?
  c. Is any indication given as to teaching sequences for units or parts of the material destined for the learners?
  d. Is the guidance given on teaching procedures clear, or is it rather vague?
  e. Is guidance given on how to set up alternative modes of activity and learning for the learners? Or is only one mode assumed?
  f. Do you think you could teach with the materials using only the teacher's book to assist you in formulating lesson plans?
  (Based on Coleman 1985)

Interpretation

Compare the teacher's and the students' books. Is there a prescribed method of teaching with the materials and for learners to work through the materials?

Or are teachers and learners free to interpret the materials and use them as they prefer?
You can draw your own conclusions if the teacher's guide contains only a list of answers to the exercises.

Action
You may have to get together with a group of colleagues and work out ways of using the material in the classroom if there is insufficient or inflexible guidance.
To monitor the effects of your procedures, see Tasks 59 and 69.

▶ TASK 68

Aim
To observe teacher and learner roles when resources such as video, audio tape, etc. are being used in the classroom.

Procedure
1 Choose to observe a class in which a colleague is using support media in the lesson. Agree to let your colleague observe a lesson when you are using support media.
2 Observation checklist. Note the following:

   a. What type(s) of task does the teacher set on the material—are they closed or open?
   b. What are the learner modes when the material is being processed and when tasks are being carried out?
   c. Does the medium lead or support a teaching point?
   d. Is the medium used to provoke speculation or is it the basis of 'content'?
   e. What is the level of learner involvement with the material?
   f. Is the material from an authentic source such as the radio or television or has it been specially prepared for language teaching purposes? Does its origin affect the teaching/learning process in terms of what the learners can contribute from their background knowledge?
   g. Does the material replace or supplement the teacher's role as informant about the target language?

Interpretation
Is learner involvement in lessons affected by the choice of support materials?
Is learner mode of work suited to the medium being used?
Is the material generative or simply a sample of language to exemplify certain language points?

Action
Experiment with new working modes with support media and monitor the effects on learner involvement (see Task 59). Experiment with new task

types with support media and observe their effect on learner processes (see Tasks 66 and 69).

Evaluate the stock of support materials in your institution and assess its suitability for different types of learning task and learner mode (see Task 66).

▶ TASK 69

Aim

To observe the effects on teacher and learner role of using new teaching materials in the classroom.

Procedure

1 Add a new piece of material or learning task to the material you plan to use in a lesson. It may be a task involving problem-solving or a task involving the use of new modes of questioning.

2 Ask a colleague to observe you while you teach and to note the following:

> What is the level of the learners' affective involvement in the task, i.e. their response to the new idea? For example, do they seem to be enjoying the task?

> Does the new material lead to greater co-operation among the learners, even if the teacher does not plan for this to occur?

> Does the teacher teach *with* or *through* the material? i.e. Does the teacher follow any pattern set up by the material or does the teacher use the material to generate classroom activity of different types?

> What is the quality of the linguistic outcome with the new material?

3 Write down your own impressions soon after the class and compare them with those of your colleague.

4 Ask some of the learners their opinions about the new material.

5 Ask the class to respond to this short questionnaire.

> Did you enjoy using _____ ? (enter title)?   YES/NO
>
> Did you feel you learnt more than usual with _____?   YES/NO
>
> Would you like to use _____ again?   YES/NO
>
> Would you like to work with _____ in a different way from the one we used in class today?   YES/NO
>
> What did you find most interesting and challenging with the new material?_____ _____ _____
>
> What did you find unusual/boring about the new material?_____
>
> _____ _____ _____

Interpretation

Depending on the response you got from the questionnaire and from your fellow teacher's observation, you will now be in a position to know whether or not to use the material again or whether or not you will have to modify aspects of it.

If the material involved you in a totally new role, did this seem to upset the students in any way?

If the material involved the learners in new roles, do you think this made any difference to the class's response? If so, in what ways?

Action

Introduce further material into the class 'menu' and monitor it in the same way.

Vary the working modes with the materials until you find an optimum pay-off in the class. (See Task 59.)

Ask colleagues to trial the material or ideas and compare your notes. Do you think that any differences between your results and theirs are due to differences in teaching style?

6 Setting up your own investigations

How do we focus on problems and issues that *we* want to investigate?
What is the best means for investigating our particular questions?
How do we collect data and material on our particular question?
How do we interpret and act upon what we have found out?

These four questions are the main concern in this section.

6.1 Finding a topic to investigate

► TASK 70

If you made notes during your reading of either Section One or Section Two, return to these.
What problems and issues did you note?
Let's now try to put these problems and observations into perspective in a more systematic way.
First: your starting point needn't actually be a problem. It may be a vague perception that something's up. Look at the checklist that follows: the items are all issues from the area of teacher and learner role. Do any of them strike a chord with you?

> Your learners' motivation
> Individual differences between learners
> Learner strategies
> Cohesiveness of the learning group
> Patterns of communication in the classroom
> Control and discipline in the learning group
> Leadership in the classroom
> Attitudes towards learning a second or foreign language
> Cultural beliefs about knowledge and its acquisition
> The modes of instruction at your disposal
> Your personal teaching style
> The textbooks and materials at your disposal

Whatever interests you, ask yourself these questions and write down your thoughts as they occur to you.

What is the present situation?
In what way(s) is this a problem?
What are the issues that we must confront in this area?
What can I (or my working group) do about it?

Your answers might look something like this:

... is a problem in my class.
I just don't know how to begin to find out about ...
... has worried me for a long time. What on earth can I do about it?
I would like to be able to ...
I don't understand ...
I have an idea about ... but I don't know how to apply it.
(Based on Hopkins 1985)

You now have some raw material to work on. The first thing to do is to evaluate your concerns in terms of their usefulness to you and your fellow teachers, your learners' potential contributions to their solution and the feasibility of actually being able to do any worthwhile research on your topic.

Some guidelines for you to consider:

1 Ask yourself the following questions:
Can I actually do anything about this matter?
What sort of scale can I work on? (i.e. How big an undertaking is my investigation going to be?)
Is the topic of interest to my institution or students?

2 Problems need investigating.
By identifying various problems and unknowns you have to all intents and purposes identified an investigation that you can do. The world in which you teach is not perfect; somehow there is a gap between what you think is ideal and what actually happens every day. For example, students are supposed to behave properly, but they don't. This shows a gap between what students are supposed to do and what they actually do. It is this sort of gap that is worth examining.
Day-to-day classroom life is probably the best starting point for your investigations.
How far are you prepared to take part in such an investigation, in which your own behaviour may be a source of data?

Working with others

If you are, at this stage, working on your own, stop and consider your position. Can you carry out your investigation without the help of colleagues or your learners? Do you feel confident enough to work on your own—do you risk adverse comment or opposition? If you have answered 'no' to either of these questions, you may feel happier working in collaboration with friends or colleagues. (If you have been working all along with a small group, this section may not really concern you, although you may be able to find ways of improving your working practices or relationships.) If you do form a group, at the outset, do the following:

1 Set goals. These may be short- or long-term.
2 Draw up an agenda for group action. Be prepared to put your priorities down the list because the answers to your questions may depend on others' work which you could help with.
3 Keep a record of your group's meetings. If you have never worked together before, you may like to investigate your group's dynamics and evolution. (See 2.3 for ideas on the sorts of events to take note of and evaluate.)
4 Be prepared to change your priorities if things go wrong, or you find that the work you are doing is producing questions to which answers are needed before the main thrust of the work can continue.

How shall I formulate my question?

There are a number of methods we can use to investigate classroom processes. The method we actually choose will depend greatly on the type of question we have asked.

Is the question you want to ask one which has grown out of your own experience in the classroom, or is it one that is already in existence or has been defined by other teachers/investigators? Let us illustrate this:

> Question A: What can we do about students who are reluctant to participate in certain types of activity?
>
> Question B: I have noticed that there are certain students who do not participate in certain activities. This is probably because they do not perceive these activities to be in line with their roles as learners. Is this so?

Question A is *open-ended*. We have identified a problem but not given any indication of what its cause might be. Our line of research would lead us to raising further questions and hinting at possible causes and courses of action that we might take.

Question B is *closed*. Not only has the problem been identified but a possible cause has been identified too. Our research would be to find out if the suggested answer was the correct one and, if it was not, then to think about alternative suggestions.

The first type of question is likely to give rise to further questions. It is, by its very nature, *generative*. The second type of question has a much narrower focus. Although it might eventually generate further questions, that is not its primary aim, which is to test our original hypothesis. We must be aware from the outset of the type of question we are asking and its potential answers or results. Above all, we must at all times be ready to question our own motives.

▶ TASK 71

Now return to the questions you have formulated in Task 70.

1 Is the question open or closed?

2 Have you thought of possible answers or explanations to your question?

3 Explore your motives: do you want to try to confirm what you have for some time thought to be the case? Or do you want to explore new possibilities?

4 Do you hope to find out something that will have an immediate pay-off in terms of normal classroom activity, or are you hoping to find out something with longer-term effects?

Having answered these questions, you should now be in a position to phrase your question more precisely, and with the knowledge that you know exactly what you are looking for in terms of answers.

Some points to note: although you may feel powerless in terms of 'changing the system' where you work, it is possible to show that by being in control of one's own teaching and classroom work, one is interpreting the system in a more productive and fruitful way. It may even turn out that desires to change things may stem from a dissatisfaction with one's own classroom performance or the way in which the learning materials one uses are written. By actually investigating the reality of classroom life, teachers may be contributing both to their own development and to the development of the system as a whole.

One thing to remember is that by putting your own teaching under scrutiny you are doing no more than extending the sorts of informal evaluation that go on in most staffrooms day in day out. Above all, there is no obligation to change one's ways—we only change if we think that it will be of benefit to ourselves or our learners.

6.2 Making a start

For your initial investigation, it would probably be advisable to settle for something that will have fairly rapid results in terms of time expended. It is probably better to build up experience and confidence over a series of short projects than to undertake a long and possibly inconclusive one.

The following is intended as a *guide* only. You are free to ignore it and choose your own way of going about things, or to adapt it as you see fit.

What is your problem or question? State it as concisely as you can. Are you going to undertake your investigation in conjunction with a colleague or alone?

What is your preferred method of collecting data? Have you the means to do this? Will it be culturally acceptable?

Will your learners be aware that the investigation is going on? Will
they be willing participants?

Is your question open or closed?

6.3 Collecting data: summary of methods

1 Questionnaires
2 Observation of lessons
3 Diary-keeping
4 Tape recording lessons
5 Interviews with participants
6 Video recording of lessons

You can also look at companion books in *Language Teaching: A Scheme
for Teacher Education*, in particular *Classroom Interaction*, for other ideas
on gathering and interpreting data in the classroom.

An interesting strategy would be to try some of these new ideas in the tasks
in Section Three as the basis for investigating the effects of tasks or the
introduction of new materials on the teacher's and learner's role. (See
Tasks 56, 59, 61, 62, 63, 64, 65, **66**, 68, **69**—tasks in bold are particularly
suitable.)

6.4 Interpreting your results

What is the meaning of the data that you have collected?
What do they tell you about your current practice in the classroom?
What do they tell you about your role as a teacher?
What do they tell you about learners' roles in your classroom?
Has your original question been answered in any way?
Can you see new questions emerging from your work?

First of all allow time to think about what you have been doing. Let your
data work for you. Brainstorming sessions with your colleagues on the
basis of the data will prove very valuable at this stage. Further questions
will undoubtedly arise from these sessions. One thing you must not worry
about is time. Set yourself reasonable targets in view of your teaching load
and regular duties. One of the great advantages of doing your own
investigations is that you can set the deadlines. Be realistic.

Special notes

Interpreting data collected on audio tape, video tape, or through interviews
Transcripts of audio tape reveal a vast amount of information about
classroom events. How objective, though, are our interpretations in the
absence of expert advice and judgement? One way of verifying one's
feelings about the data on transcripts is to do triangulation. This is a form

of interviewing where you find out the perceptions of one or more of the participants in the event you have recorded. You need only ask a limited number of questions, such as:

> What did you mean when you said . . .?
> Did you intend . . . to happen?
> Was this (identify event) what you expected to happen?
> Were you aware of (identify event or trend) during the lesson?

Each of these questions is likely to lead to a number of other questions directed towards a clarification of the event you have isolated from the transcript. The process is best carried out immediately after the class in question so that events are as fresh in the memory as possible. Triangulation can therefore be carried out both immediately after the event or some time later. If the participants are not available for comment, another teacher can provide valuable insights into your data. All of these impressions build up a fuller picture and by so doing give weight to your findings.

Interpreting questionnaires

How much weight can we give to the responses to questionnaires? Much depends on how large the sample is, but it is possible, even without sophisticated statistical techniques, to establish general trends in a group of respondents. The evidence gains strength if the sample is both large enough and representative enough.

Provided that the questionnaire can be answered on a yes/no basis, the trends which are very strong, i.e. with 60% in favour of either alternative, triangulation and further questionnaires can be administered in order to establish the validity of the trends.

Making sense of it all

Whenever you have finished collecting material on your classroom and the activities that go on in there, you have to act. This does not necessarily mean that you have to change everything you do and start afresh. Such a course would probably be so radical that your learners' expectations would be severely disappointed, unless, that is, that they were involved in an appreciation of what the changes meant for them.

In other words, you cannot make sense of your situation without the perspectives of the learners being taken into account. While they might not necessarily be taking part in the design of the research, they may be a rich source of opinion and counterpoint to the work you undertake. As well as scrutinizing your teaching, you should also be helping the learners to put their learning under the microscope and become better learners in the process.

How do you feel about this idea of letting the learners participate in your investigations? Do you think that learners can become better learners? What might this involve? (See 4.1 for ideas on this subject.) Some questions to ask of your data and methods:

1 What is significant about what I have found out in terms of the roles of teacher and learner?
2 Does what I have found involve a re-think on my part?
3 Can the situation, if it is undesirable, be changed in any way?
4 Have I found out anything new about teacher and learner role in my situation? If it is significant or new, how do I tell people outside my own working situation? Who do I tell?
5 How do I let my learners know what I am doing, and what I have found out? Should I actually take this course of action?
6 How long do I wait before I do more investigations on this subject?

Sharing your results

You might, at this stage, feel that the results of your work are negligible, too insignificant to worry about. This could never be so. We do not know enough about what goes on in classrooms where second languages are being taught to dismiss even the smallest detail. Everything that we as teachers and learners find out is potentially relevant. The only way in which to prove this to oneself is to share it with like-minded people, both fellow professionals and anyone else in the teacher/learner role set who can be persuaded to listen.

Spreading the news

We need to circulate our findings in some way.

We can choose to circulate our findings informally in 'staff development' meetings with our immediate colleagues. In this way you can get immediate feedback from people working in your own working environment.

If there is a teachers' association or a similar organization in your area, this might provide a useful venue for letting a larger number of people know what we have done and for subjecting our work to a greater degree of criticism, either formally or informally.

A most commonly accepted means of circulating our results formally is to put them in a short written report. A reasonably simple format is as follows:

1 State the problem or the set of circumstances that you set out to investigate.

2 Describe briefly how you collected your data and how you interpreted them.

3 State what action you are taking as a result of this.

4 Outline the implications in terms of teacher and learner role in your classroom and what you intend to do with regard to your current set of practices.

5 Evaluate the effectiveness of the research procedure and say what you might do differently next time.

Even if you do not write reports on your investigations, at least discuss them with colleagues, your students and anyone else who is prepared to listen.

The more we know about what happens in classrooms, the better the process inside can be made and perhaps even the end result, in terms of more efficient and enjoyable language learning.

Glossary

affective: describing the emotional side of a social encounter—or affect—in contrast to the cognitive, or mental, side.

closed task: a task where there is only one correct answer possible.

coercive power: power imposed by force or by threat of force.

content-oriented: a way of describing a learning activity to indicate that the acquisition of knowledge is the main goal.

convention: a procedure for conducting social activities agreed upon by those who engage in them.

instruction: teaching behaviour aimed at transferring knowledge to learners (c.f. management).

instrumental motivation: motivation inspired by the promise of reward or betterment.

integrative motivation: motivation believed to lead a language learner to want to become a part of the community whose language is being learnt.

interactivity: a way of describing a learning activity in terms of its potential for interaction between learners. It can be high or low.

interpersonality: a way of describing a learning activity in terms of its potential for engaging a learner affectively. Learning activities thus range from experiential—high level of interpersonality—to instrumental.

learning strategies: ways in which learners seek to control learning opportunities either cognitively or through social interaction in the learning group.

learning style: behaviour which indicates the ways in which learners participate in group learning activities.

management: teaching or learning behaviour aimed at organizing learning and learning activities (c.f. instruction).

norm: behaviour or standard of behaviour accepted by a social group. Agreed ways of carrying out social activities.

open-ended task: a task for which a variety of solutions is possible.

organizational network: communication pattern developed by a small group engaged in a problem-solving task.

personality profile: an assessment of an individual's personality based on a series of behavioural characteristics.

position: occupation; usually ranked if in an organization.

procedural topic: that part of verbal interaction related to the conduct of the interaction.

process-oriented: way of describing a learning activity to show that the social interaction between the participants is the main goal.

referent power: power exercised by appealing to people's respect and support of an organization.

reward-based power: power exercised by means of appeal to people's desires for reward for action, e.g. the offering of bonuses for extra work.

role conflict: condition where an individual is unsure of what his or her precise role is in an organization or social relationship.

role expectations: one's expectations of the appropriate behaviour of an individual in a given role.

role network: relationships between different roles in an organization.

role relationship: behaviour of individuals when cast in opposing or complementary roles.

role set: individuals and groups who influence the behaviour of a role holder.

social distance: feeling of ease or uneasiness when in social contact with individuals. Strongly influenced by knowledge of status.

status: relative social prominence.

teaching strategies: ways of organizing instruction to promote learning.

teaching style: teaching behaviour which is the result of the combination of organizational and personal qualities.

Further reading

Argyle, M. 1969. *Social Interaction*. London: Tavistock Press.
Argyle's volume covers all the aspects of human social interaction which influence role behaviour.

Barnes, D. 1976. *From Communication to Curriculum*. Harmondsworth: Penguin Books.
This book is required reading for people interested in the teacher/learner relationship. It concentrates on the modes of communication found in classrooms.

Candlin, C. N. and C. Edelhoff. 1982. *Challenges: Teacher's Book*. Harlow: Longman.
This teacher's guide is an excellent source of teaching ideas beyond the materials for which it was written. Worth looking at for the statement of principles at the beginning.

Cohen, L. and L. Manion. 1981. *Perspectives on Classrooms and Schools*. London: Holt, Rinehart, and Winston.
A comprehensive survey of every major topic in education. The first five chapters are particularly relevant to an understanding of teacher and learner roles.

Cunningsworth, A. 1984. *Evaluating and Selecting EFL Teaching Materials*. London: Heinemann Educational Books.
A consumer guide to teaching materials. It raises useful points about the views of methodology implicit in many coursebooks.

Littlewood, W. 1981. *The Communicative Teaching of English*. Cambridge: Cambridge University Press.
A lucid introduction to the communicative approach with interesting and practical teaching ideas.

Malamah-Thomas, A. 1987. *Classroom Interaction*. Oxford: Oxford University Press.
Classroom Interaction mediates between teaching and learning. The purpose of the book is to examine this interaction and to explore its pedagogic implications.

McLeish, J. 1973. *The Psychology of the Learning Group*. London: Hutchinson.
An important book which discusses the social psychology of teacher and learner role.

Morrison, A. and D. McIntyre. 1973. Second edition. *Teachers and Teaching*. Harmondsworth: Penguin Books.
An excellent survey of the managerial and instructional aspects of the teacher's role.

Riley, P. (ed.). 1984. *Discourse and Learning*. Harlow: Longman.
This volume contains many original and interesting articles which have a bearing on teacher and learner roles.

Rivers, W. 1981. Second edition. *Teaching Foreign-Language Skills.*. Chicago and London: Chicago University Press.
A classic survey of language teaching methods, with discussion questions and exercises for readers.

Walker, R. and C. Adelman. 1975. *A Guide to Classroom Observation*. London: Methuen.
An original and interesting volume for trainee teachers on ways of observing classroom life.

Bibliography

Abbott, G. and P. Wingard. 1981. *Teaching English as an International Language.* London: Collins.

Abbs, B., C. N. Candlin, C. Edelhoff, T. Moston, and M. Sexton. 1981. Third impression. *Challenges: Student's Book.* Harlow: Longman.

Abbs, B. and I. Freebairn. 1979. *Developing Strategies. Student's Book.* Harlow: Longman.

Abbs, B. and I. Freebairn. 1984. *Building Strategies: Student's Book.* Harlow: Longman.

Allwright, R. A. 1981. 'What do we need teaching materials for?' *ELT Journal* Vol 36 No 1.

Allwright, R. A. 1984. 'The importance of interaction in the classroom'. *Applied Linguistics* Vol 5 No 2.

Argyle, M. 1969. *Social Interaction.* London: Tavistock Press.

Barnes, D. 1969. 'Language in the secondary school classroom,' in D. Barnes, J. Britton, and H. Rosen. *Language, the Learner and the School.* Harmondsworth: Penguin Books.

Barnes, D. 1976. *From Communication To Curriculum.* Harmondsworth: Penguin Books.

Black, V., M. McNorton, A. Malderez, and S. Parker. 1986. *Fast Forward 1: Classbook.* Oxford: Oxford University Press.

Breen, M. P. and C. N. Candlin. 1980. 'The essentials of a communicative curriculum in language teaching'. *Applied Linguistics* Vol 1 No 2.

Breen, M. P. and C. N. Candlin. 1987. 'Which Materials? A Consumer's and Designer's Guide' in L. Sheldon (ed.) *Textbook and Materials Evaluation.* ELT Documents. The British Council.

Brumfit, C. 1980. *Problems and Principles in English Language Teaching.* Oxford: Pergamon Press.

Brumfit, C. 1981. Review of G. Moskovitz. 1978. *Caring and Sharing In the Foreign Language Class. ELT Journal* Vol 36 No 1.

Candlin, C. N. and C. Edelhoff. 1982. *Challenges: Teacher's Handbook.* Harlow: Longman.

Cohen, L. and L. Manion. 1980. *Research Methods in Education.* London: Croom Helm.

Cohen, L. and L. Manion. 1981. *Perspectives on Classrooms and Schools.* London: Holt, Rinehart, and Winston.

Coleman, H. 1985. 'Evaluating teachers' guides. Do teachers' guides guide teachers?' in J. C. Alderson (ed.) *Evaluation.* Practical Papers in English Language Education Vol 6. Oxford: Pergamon Press.

Cortis, G. 1977. *The Social Context of Teaching.* London: Open Books.

Cunningsworth, A. 1984. *Evaluating and Selecting EFL Teaching Materials.* London: Heinemann Educational Books.

Dan, L. 1983. *Beginning English.* Mimeo. Denmark: Greve Kommune.

Delamont, S. 1983. Second edition. *Interaction In The Classroom.* London: Methuen.

Doff, A., C. Jones and K. Mitchell. 1983. *Meanings Into Words Intermediate.* Cambridge: Cambridge University Press.

Dykstra, G. 1978. 'Today's Curriculum for Tomorrow's World.' Mimeo. University of Hawaii at Manoa.

Edwards, A. D. 1976. *Language In Culture and Class.* London: Heinemann Educational Books.

Evans, K. M. 1978. *Planning Small-Scale Research.* Windsor: National Foundation for Educational Research.

Frank, C., M. Rinvolucri, and M. Berer. 1982. *Challenge To Think.* Oxford: Oxford University Press.

Gibson, T. 1973. *Teachers Talking.* Quoted in Delamont 1983.

Giles, H. and J. L. Byrne. 1982. 'An Intergroup Approach To Second Language Acquisition'. *Journal of Multilingual and Multicultural Development* Vol 3 No 1.

Goffman, E. 1981. *Forms of Talk.* Oxford: Blackwell.

Gower, R. and S. Walters. 1983. *A Teaching Practice Handbook.* London: Heinemann Educational Books.

Grellet, F. 1983. *Developing Reading Skills.* Cambridge: Cambridge University Press.

Grellet, F., A. Maley, and W. Welsing. 1982. *Quartet 1:* Teacher's Book. Oxford: Oxford University Press.

Gremmo, M. and D. Abé. 1985 in Riley, P. (ed.) *Discourse and Learning.* Harlow: Longman.

Harmer, J. 1983. *The Practice of English Language Teaching.* Harlow: Longman.

Hartley, B. and P. Viney. 1982. *Streamline English Connections.* Oxford: Oxford University Press.

Haycraft, J. 1978. *An Introduction To English Language Teaching.* Harlow: Longman.

Hedge, T. and H. M. Dobinson. 1982. *What's The Problem?* London: Thomas Nelson.

Henderson, M. and M. Argyle. 1984. 'Endorsed and applied rules of relationships reported by teachers.' *Oxford Review of Education* Vol 10 No 4.

Hill, L. A. and M. Dobbyn. 1982. *A Teacher Training Handbook.* London: Cassell.

Hopkins, D. 1985. *A Teacher's Guide To Classroom Research.* Milton Keynes: Open University Press.

Hubbard, P., H. Jones, B. Thornton, and R. Wheeler. 1983. *A Training Course For TEFL.* Oxford: Oxford University Press.

Jackson, P. 1968. *Life In Classrooms*. New York: Holt, Rinehart, and Winston.

Johnson, K. and K. Morrow. 1981. *Communication In The Classroom*. Harlow: Longman.

Jones, L. 1981. *Functions Of English*. Cambridge: Cambridge University Press.

Jones, L. 1984. *Ideas*. Cambridge: Cambridge University Press.

Klippel, F. 1984. *Keep Talking*. Cambridge: Cambridge University Press.

Langenheim, L. 1980. 'Am I me?—Roleplay for intermediate to advanced students' in Spaventa (ed.) 1980.

Leavitt, H. J. 1951. 'Some effects of certain communication patterns on group performance.' *Journal of Abnormal Social Psychology* Vol 46.

Lemlich, J. K. 1979. *Classroom Management*. New York: Harper and Row.

Lewis, R. G. 1984. *Advance Your English*. London: Hodder and Stoughton.

Littlejohn, A. 1985. 'Learner choice in language study.' *ELT Journal* Vol 39 No 4.

Littlewood, W. 1981. *The Communicative Teaching of English*. Cambridge: Cambridge University Press.

Maley, A. and A. Duff. 1978. *Drama Techniques In Language Learning*. Cambridge: Cambridge University Press.

Maley, A., A. Duff, and F. Grellet. 1980. *The Mind's Eye*. Cambridge: Cambridge University Press.

Maslow, A. H. 1968. *Towards A Psychology of Being*. Second edition. Princeton: Van Nostrad.

McGregor, D. M. 1960. *The Human Side of Enterprise*. New York: McGraw-Hill.

McLeish, J. 1973. *The Psychology of The Learning Group*. London: Hutchinson.

Millington-Ward, J. 1972. *Practice In Structure and Usage*. Harlow: Longman.

Moore, J. (British Council director of the project) 1979. *Reading and Thinking in English: Discovering Discourse*. The British Council. Oxford: Oxford University Press.

Morrison, A. and D. McIntyre. 1972. *The Social Psychology of Teaching*. Harmondsworth: Penguin Books.

Morrison, A. and D. McIntyre. 1973. Second edition. *Teachers and Teaching*. Harmondsworth: Penguin Books.

Naipaul, S. 1984. *Beyond The Dragon's Mouth*. London: Hamish Hamilton.

Nicholls, S. and J. Naish. 1981. *Teaching English As A Second Language*. London: BBC Publications.

O'Neill, R., R. Kingsbury, T. Yeadon and R. Scott. 1971a. *Kernel Lessons Intermediate*. Student's Book. Harlow: Longman.

O'Neill, R., R. Kingsbury, T. Yeadon and R. Scott. 1971b. *Kernel Lessons Intermediate*. Teacher's Book. Harlow: Longman.

Perry, W. G. 1968 *Forms of Intellectual and Ethical Development in the College Years.* New York: Holt, Rinehart, and Winston.

Porter Ladousse, G. 1983. *Speaking Personally.* Cambridge: Cambridge University Press.

Raban, J. 1979. *Arabia Through The Looking Glass.* London: Collins.

Riley, P. (ed.). 1985. *Discourse and Learning.* Harlow: Longman.

Rinvolucri, M. 1980. 'Teacherless tasks' in Spaventa (ed.) 1980.

Rinvolucri, M. 1984. *Grammar Games.* Cambridge: Cambridge University Press.

Rivers, W. 1981. *Teaching Foreign-Language Skills.* Second edition. Chicago and London: Chicago University Press.

Rudzka, B., J. Channel, Y. Putseys, and P. Ostyn. 1981. *The Words You Need.* London: Macmillan.

Salimbene, S. 1981. 'Non-frontal teaching methodology.' *ELT Journal* Vol 35 No 2.

Schmuck, R. A. and P. A. Schmuck. 1976. *Group Processes In The Classroom.* San Francisco: Wm C Brown.

Sinclair, J. McH. and D. Brazil. 1982. *Teacher Talk.* Oxford: Oxford University Press.

Spaventa, L. (ed.). 1980. *Towards The Creative Teaching Of English.* London: Allen and Unwin.

Stenhouse, L. 1975. *An Introduction To Curriculum Research and Development.* London: Heinemann Educational Books.

Stevick, E. W. 1980. *Teaching Languages: A Way and Ways.* Rowley, Mass: Newbury House.

Swan, M. and C. Walter. 1985. *The Cambridge English Course Book 2. Teacher's Book.* Cambridge: Cambridge University Press.

Thomson, A. J. and A. V. Martinet. 1986. *A Practical English Grammar: Exercises 1.* Oxford: Oxford University Press.

Ur, P. 1981. *Discussions That Work.* Cambridge: Cambridge University Press.

Walker, R. and C. Adelman. 1975. *A Guide To Classroom Observation.* London: Methuen.

Wallerstein, N. 1983. *Language and Culture In Conflict.* New York: Addison Wesley.

Widdowson, H. G. 1978. *Teaching Language As Communication.* Oxford: Oxford University Press.

Williams, R. 1982. *Panorama.* Harlow: Longman.

Willis, J. 1981. *Teaching English Through English.* Harlow: Longman.

Wright, A. D. 'Language Teaching and Learning: Analysis of an Activity Type.' PhD Thesis. University of Lancaster. (In preparation).